## Contents

| | | |
|---|---|---|
| 1 | Follow Sound Doctrine *1 Timothy 1:1-11* | **5** |
| 2 | God's Grace Overflows *1 Timothy 1:12-20* | **14** |
| 3 | How to Act in Church *1 Timothy 2:1-15* | **24** |
| 4 | Qualifications for Leaders *1 Timothy 3:1-16* | **34** |
| 5 | How to Deal With False Doctrine *1 Timothy 4:1-16* | **44** |
| 6 | How to Treat Others *1 Timothy 5:1 to 6:2* | **53** |
| 7 | Quest for True Wealth *1 Timothy 6:3-21* | **63** |
| 8 | Encouragement to Faithfulness *2 Timothy 1:1-18* | **72** |
| 9 | Rewards of Faithfulness *2 Timothy 2:1-13* | **81** |
| 10 | How to Be God's Man *2 Timothy 2:14-26* | **91** |
| 11 | Trends of the Times *2 Timothy 3:1-13* | **100** |
| 12 | The Value of Scripture *2 Timothy 3:14 to 4:5* | **109** |
| 13 | Foes, Friends, and Final Words *2 Timothy 4:6-22* | **117** |

# GARY LEGGETT
# LETTERS TO TIMOTHY

**Radiant** BOOKS
Gospel Publishing House/Springfield, Mo. 65802

02-0877

© 1981 by the Gospel Publishing House, Springfield, Missouri 65802. All rights reserved. No part of this book may be reproduced, stored in a retrieval system, or transmitted in any form or by any means, electronic, mechanical, photocopy, recording, or otherwise, without prior written permission of the copyright owner, except brief quotations used in connection with reviews in magazines or newspapers.

Library of Congress Catalog Card Number 80-82830
International Standard Book Number 0-88243-877-8
Printed in the United States of America

A teacher's guide for individual or group study with this book is available from the Gospel Publishing House (order number 32-0189).

CHAPTER **1**

# Follow Sound Doctrine

*Read 1 Timothy 1:1-11*

HOW WOULD YOU GIVE ADVICE to somebody who lives 300 miles away? If it was urgent you could use the Bell System. Talking with that person on the telephone would give you all the information you need. Then you could respond with the necessary advice and counsel. But suppose no telephones existed. The next best means of communication probably would be a telegram or a letter. With these, a delay of a day or more, and the inability to respond immediately would slow down the process of communication. But what if there were no telegraph or mail service? Your ability to correspond and receive a reply would be greatly hampered. Very possibly you would write a lengthy letter and include all the advice you felt the situation called for, and send it by special messenger.

That's what Paul did. Because he could not visit the people and churches that needed his counsel, he wrote letters to them. As the Holy Spirit revealed to Paul the message God wanted His people to have, Paul wrote letters that included a great deal of teaching and personal counsel. Two of Paul's letters were written to a very special young man.

## "Timothy, My Son"

"Paul, an apostle of Jesus Christ by the commandment of God our Saviour, and Lord Jesus Christ, which is our hope; unto Timothy, my own son in the faith" (1 Timothy 1:1, 2).

Most of Paul's greetings follow a pattern. He names himself (and sometimes those who are with him), then declares his apostleship or servanthood. Only in three letters does he refer to someone as "son" (see 1 Timothy 1:2, 18; 2 Timothy 1:2; 2:1; Titus 1:4). This meant a special relationship existed between the apostle and a "son in the faith." So we can expect that what Paul wrote to Timothy would be special and of the "fatherly advice" type of counsel. Since God selected Paul to be an apostle of Jesus Christ, Paul's message carries the authority and genuineness of the true gospel. He wrote to Timothy to warn him about those who failed to follow sound doctrine. Paul's counsel is needed just as much today.

Who was Timothy? How did he become a co-worker with Paul? What was his ministry, and where?

To answer these questions we need to look in Acts and a few other New Testament Books to construct a biographical outline of Timothy's life.

1. His mother was a Jewess; his father was a Greek (Acts 16:1-3).

2. Paul met Timothy first in Lystra (Acts 16:1).

3. Timothy joined Paul on his second missionary journey (Acts 16:3; 17:14, 15; 18:5).

4. Timothy also traveled with Paul on the third missionary journey and was sent to Macedonia (Acts 19:22; 20:4).

5. Timothy is called a fellow worker (Romans 16:21) and a brother (2 Corinthians 1:1; Colossians 1:1; Philemon 1).

6. Timothy was sent to Corinth to correct errors among believers (1 Corinthians 4:17; 16:10).

7. Paul sent Timothy to Thessalonica to help the

church and bring back a progress report (1 Thessalonians 3:2, 6).

8. Hebrews 13:23 reports that Timothy had been set free from prison.

9. Paul left Timothy in Ephesus to deal with false teachers (1 Timothy 1:3).

10. Perhaps Paul's highest commendation regarding Timothy is found in Philippians 2:19-22, especially the final words: "...as a son with the father, he hath served with me in the gospel."

Timothy was a young man who could be trusted. He had proved faithful in many situations. Like a soldier he could take orders and be sent anywhere. Most of his ministry was on the "front lines"—with Paul in his dangerous missionary journeys and as an arbitrator in churches with problems. In Paul's second letter to Timothy, Paul referred to him as "...a good soldier of Jesus Christ" (2 Timothy 2:3).

A son and a soldier: what a combination! But just as Paul had a son in the faith, so God has "Timothys" today. As God's sons and daughters who claim Jesus as the Captain of our faith, we can go forth in the power of the Spirit to win victories for our Lord. Jesus is our greatest example of how we should serve.

## "Grace, Mercy, and Peace"

All of Paul's letters include a formal salutation similar to this style found in Timothy. The difference in the letters to Timothy and Titus is the addition of the word *mercy*. Let's look at these three words.

1. *Grace* contains two ideas in the New Testament: undeserved generosity and God-ordained universality. The salvation of those who believe is God's work and not man's. God invites "whosoever will" to come. Ephe-

sians 2:8, 9 shows the extent and effect of God's grace.

2. *Mercy* contains the Old Testament idea of lovingkindness or steadfast love. Perhaps Paul included this word in his greeting to encourage Timothy. He was in a tight spot and needed God's help. As Timothy reflected on God's mercy, he would be encouraged to lean upon the Lord in his present circumstances.

3. *Peace* is the usual greeting in the East. But God's peace is more than the absence of trouble—it is a tranquillity and a sense of well-being that comes from knowing God. When we are "in Him" we have perfect peace.

More important than the form of the greeting, however, is the source of these wonderful blessings. Note how the Holy Spirit guides Paul as he describes God and Christ:

| | |
|---|---|
| God our Saviour,<br>Lord Jesus Christ, our hope | 1 Timothy 1:1 |
| God the Father,<br>Jesus Christ our Lord | 2 Timothy 1:2 |

These four concepts form the basis of the gospel that reveals grace, mercy and peace to us. God is the only Saviour, there is no other. Jesus Christ is the only hope of reconciliation with God the Father. He is the only Mediator between God and man. Because of God's grace and mercy we can find peace with God, and the peace of God by believing on the Lord Jesus Christ. This is good news!

**Challenge False Teachers**

Paul, moved by the Holy Spirit, wastes no time in getting to the heart of the matter. False doctrine was endangering the church and he wanted Timothy to speak out against it. This heresy was identifiable by two distinct characteristics: fables (myths, idle tales) and endless genealogies. False teachers used these to promote controversies among believers. Timothy is advised to take a strong stand against the false teachers and charge (command) them to cease.

Some commentators see a reference to the heresy of Gnosticism here as well as certain other passages of the New Testament. But it seems these false teachers were Judaizers, not Gnostics. Fables and genealogies were a favorite pastime of certain Jews who delighted in embellishing the text of the Old Testament and bringing others under condemnation with fabricated laws.

The church today must guard against modern "Judaizers" who want to teach false doctrine and promote controversy. These false teachers must be challenged with the truth of the glorious gospel of God (v. 11). Truth and error cannot coexist. God is looking for a son or daughter in the faith who will stand up and "... command certain men not to teach false doctrines any longer" (v. 3, *New International Version*).

## Commanded to Love

First Timothy 1:5 introduces a basic precept of the gospel: love. This love is to come from (1) a pure heart, (2) a good conscience, and (3) sincere faith. First, Christian love must come from the heart which is the seat of the emotions and will. That heart must be pure if the love is to be genuine and effective. Note Jesus' promise to the pure in heart in Matthew 5:8.

Second, Christian love must come from a good conscience. We know the purpose of conscience: to help us know right from wrong. But a person's conscience can be tempered by many things. It can be pure and good, but it can also be seared and defiled (compare Acts 23:1; Hebrews 13:18; 1 Timothy 3:9; 4:2; Titus 1:15). The Biblical conscience implies moral sense "... to discern both good and evil" (Hebrews 5:14). Letting your conscience be your guide can be devastating unless that conscience has been redirected to the good and pure by the Holy Spirit.

Finally, Christian love must come from sincere faith. These false teachers in Ephesus could pretend to hold to the true faith, but their actions proved differently. Promoting controversies that did not edify, they displayed the insincerity of their own false belief. Those who want others to come to the truth must demonstrate a love that finds its source in genuine faith.

Love is not a new command for the Christian. Jesus summed up the whole Law with two commands: "Thou shalt love the Lord thy God ... and ... thy neighbor as thyself" (Mark 12:30, 31). He also said, "By this shall all men know that ye are my disciples, if ye have love one to another" (John 13:35). Paul gives a beautiful discourse on love in 1 Corinthians 13, describing its attributes and actions. It's worth the minute and a half to read it right now.

The kind of love Paul is speaking of here is *agape*, God's love. It is easy to love those who love us. But what about those who don't care for us, or who oppose us? Jesus had a word for this situation too: "Love your enemies, bless them that curse you, do good to them that hate you, and pray for them which despitefully use you, and persecute you" (Matthew 5:44).

Timothy's rebuke of these false teachers must be done with love as his motivation. Though they had left sound doctrine and wandered away from the truth, Timothy is to love them as people while charging their actions as wrong and worthy of public rebuke. Personal animosity has no place in the Christian's attitudes and relationships. Every person who names the name of Christ is obligated to act as He would in any given situation. And that is always in love.

## Empty Talk From Ignorant Teachers

*Vain jangling* is a very interesting term. As we read the context it seems to be the primary characteristic and activity of these false teachers. Paul points out that fables and endless genealogies are their stock in trade. He calls it meaningless discussion, empty argument, and purposeless talk. He also says they have turned aside from the truth and are so ignorant that they can't even understand their own words (v. 7).

The truths of the gospel are both simple and profound. We can be guilty of communicating on the pseudo intellectual level of eternal truth. Even if it does not degenerate into falsehood, it can become "vain jangling" that is void of love and does not edify. Let us ask God to give us the good sense and spiritual insight to speak the truth in love (Ephesians 4:15) and to keep it simple!

## The Law and the Lawless

"'Stay Alive at 55' Is More Than a Slogan, It's the Law!" The billboard announcement sought to do two things: inform and deter. Every driver in the U.S. knows the speed limit on open highways is 55 MPH. Yet a news article seen at the time of this writing contained the following: "State police speeding arrests in _____ last month totaled 12,363, the highest monthly total so far this year, Department of Public Safety figures showed Monday." The article went on to report that 2,675 arrests were for violations in the 56-65 MPH range; 8,427 in the 66-75 MPH range; 1,296 for 76-90 MPH; and 65 for speeds greater than 90 MPH. It is evident that drivers know the limits of speed laws, but they are not willing to keep them.

Paul's letter to Timothy picks up this theme of law in verses 8 and 9. The uniqueness of Paul's inspired counsel is the fact that he is writing about God's law. He makes two points very clear: (1) God's law is good if it is used properly, and (2) laws are not made for righteous men but for unrighteous men. Paul then gives a list of lawbreakers in verses 9 and 10. This list greatly resembles the Ten Commandments in Exodus 20:1-17. Note how the Holy Spirit directs Paul to link several of these in pairs and how they align with certain of the Commandments. (For example: "unholy and profane" and the Third and Fourth Commandments have a definite comparison.)

### Sound Doctrine and the Gospel

Finally, Paul adds the words: "... and if there be any other thing that is contrary to sound doctrine" (v. 10). This makes the list complete—no unrighteous person or act is left out. This list contains some heavy sins. Paul was writing about the moral corruption in a city of the first century whose state religion was given over to vile and immoral acts. Our society seems to be rushing headlong in the same direction. The deterrent and remedy for first-century believers applies today: sound doctrine and the glorious gospel of God.

The word *sound* here literally means "health-giving" and denotes the wholesomeness or healthiness of true Christian teaching. *Gospel* means "good news." Both of these—sound doctrine and the gospel—are in extreme contrast to the fables, endless genealogies, and vain jangling of the false teachers at Ephesus. Timothy's charge is to command them to cease and desist. He is to focus on the doctrine that is wholesome and healthy and the gospel that is glorious. This gospel was committed to Paul's trust. The inference of verse 11 is that this gospel was committed to Timothy's trust as well.

This same glorious gospel is also committed to our trust. The Great Commission gives us the mandate to "go... into all the world, and preach the gospel to every creature" (Mark 16:15). Matthew adds, "Teaching them to observe all things whatsoever I [Jesus] have commanded you" (28:20). As we do this, and our families, friends, and all we reach respond to the truth, the gospel will become "the power of God unto salvation to everyone that believeth" (Romans 1:16).

## CHAPTER 2

## God's Grace Overflows

*Read 1 Timothy 1:12-20*

> *Marvelous grace of our loving Lord,*
> *Grace that exceeds our sin and our guilt,*
> *Yonder on Calvary's mount outpoured,*
> *There where the blood of the Lamb was spilt.*
>
> *Grace, grace, God's grace,*
> *Grace that will pardon and cleanse within;*
> *Grace, grace, God's grace,*
> *Grace that is greater than all our sin.*
>
> Julia H. Johnston

HALFWAY THROUGH THE FIRST CHAPTER Paul breaks forth into praise and thanksgiving for the marvelous grace of God. The apostle gives a stirring testimony of God's mercy and superabundant grace. He begins with these words: "And I thank Christ Jesus our Lord, who hath enabled me..." (1 Timothy 1:12).

As we study this section in 1 Timothy we will see God's grace in the life of Paul. And we will receive courage to trust this same grace to overflow in our lives too.

### Strengthened and Called

At the time of writing 1 Timothy (about A.D. 64) Paul had been saved for 30 years. Yet he could never get away from the fact of his miraculous conversion and call to the ministry. He had testified before governors and kings and proclaimed Christ's gospel among the Jews and gentiles. Even now, writing to a dear friend, Paul pens a hymn of praise that climaxes in a beautiful doxology (v. 17). Let's look at its significant parts.

In verse 12 Paul makes the fourth mention of Jesus Christ in these few verses. Before he gets to his doxology Paul will mention Christ three more times. Seven times in seventeen verses! The Holy Spirit inspired Paul to write this letter, and the apostle's focus rests and remains on the Lord Jesus Christ.

This vital truth should be the Christian's guide: Jesus Christ is to be the focal point of our life and witness. Are we guilty of taking the limelight when what we are, or whatever we've become is all by the grace of our Lord? Do we really give the glory to Him? He deserves our deepest gratitude and our most faithful service. He is our Lord!

Paul thanks Christ for three things: (1) strength, (2) trust, and (3) a call to service. When Paul was chosen it was no bed of roses for him. But he had learned that Christ never gives a person a task without also giving him the power and strength to do it. Paul never said, "Look what I've done," but always, "Look what Jesus Christ has enabled me to do." Second, when Christ saved this former enemy of Christians, He forgave and trusted him. Often we forgive someone who has made a mistake or sinned, but we are reluctant to trust him again with any responsibility. But Christ isn't that way. He forgives, forgets, and trusts that person implicitly.

Because Christ trusted Paul He called him into service. The King James Version brings out an important point: Christ put Paul into the ministry. Paul didn't select the ministry as a vocation, he was divinely called. Also, the word *ministry* is from the Greek *diakonia*, which basically means "service." Paul didn't think of himself as being appointed to a place of honor or a position of leadership. After 30 years of ministry, he testifies that he is saved to serve. What an example for Timothy! And what a needful reminder to all of us.

## Mercy Needed and Received

Have you noticed how fond of trilogies Paul is? When he mentions something, he usually does it in threes. Verse 13 gives us another trilogy: Paul says he was a blasphemer, a persecutor, and injurious. *Blasphemer* relates to the mouth. Paul, then Saul, probably cursed the name of Jesus. He now regards his preconversion words as blasphemy against the divine Son of God. As a *persecutor* Saul "... made havoc of the church" (Acts 8:3; compare 9:1, 2, 4 5; 22:4, 5; 26:9-11). Galatians 1:13 says he "... persecuted the church of God, and *wasted it*." Contemporary jargon has picked up this meaning. To "waste" a person is to "wipe him out." That's what Saul was doing to believers.

The word *injurious* is a strong, descriptive term. It actually means a violent, insolent man. It might include the image we have of a sadist: one who inflicts pain on another for the sheer joy of doing it.

"But I obtained mercy...." What wonderful words! They are found in verse 13 and repeated in verse 16. Take a moment to look up these verses, read them, pray for insight, and ponder them.

Mercy was given to Paul because what he did as Saul the Persecutor was done "ignorantly in unbelief." By these words Paul does not excuse his sinful past but accounts for the demonstration of God's mercy to one who was (and still is, note the present tense "am") chief of sinners (v. 15). Verse 16 then gives the purpose for this glorious mercy:

> But for that very reason I was shown mercy so that in me, the worst of sinners, Christ Jesus might display his unlimited patience as an example for those who would believe on him and receive eternal life (*New International Version*).

### God's Abundant Grace

A teacher once asked a class of primaries, "What does the word *grace* mean?" One girl said it was the name of the baby on *Little House on the Prairie*. Another, sure that she had the correct answer, declared, "It's the prayer we say at the table!"

God's grace is a Biblical truth that can be defined in finite terms, but its substance is infinite. Although it may be explained in human words, its limits are beyond comprehension. Like so many truths of the gospel, it's "better felt than telt." For Paul, "the grace of our Lord" was not just an abstract concept but an active force dominating both his thoughts and actions. He could say:

> For I am the least of the apostles, that am not meet to be called an apostle, because I persecuted the church of God. But by the grace of God I am what I am: and his grace which was bestowed upon me was not in vain; but I labored more abundantly than they all: yet not I, but the grace of God which was with me (1 Corinthians 15:9, 10).

In our text of 1 Timothy 1:14, Paul says this grace was superabundant with faith and love. Faith is one of Paul's favorite words. We have already seen it in verse 5; we will notice it several more times in these two letters to Timothy.

Someone has said of verse 14 that Paul sees "grace" as

providing for his salvation, "faith" appropriating it, and "love" applying it. Thank God that His abundant grace is still active today. Anyone who believes can experience the love, forgiveness, and cleansing that God's grace provides.

## The Heart of the Gospel

"This is a faithful saying, and worthy of all acceptation, that Christ Jesus came into the world to save sinners" (v. 15). This is the first of four statements that begin with, or contain the words, "this is a faithful saying" (see 1 Timothy 1:15; 3:1 [*true* is the same as *faithful*]; 4:8, 9; 2 Timothy 2:11). In two of the four Paul includes the words "worthy of all acceptation." We have little trouble in understanding what the Holy Spirit wants the readers of this Epistle and the second letter to do: pay attention and accept the truth.

Here the truth is doctrinal: "Christ Jesus came into the world to save sinners." It is the very heart of the gospel. The Son of God left heaven and came to earth for one purpose: to save sinners. Jesus spoke this truth in Luke 19:10: "The Son of man is come to seek and to save that which was lost." No greater truth exists. Jesus came to save sinners. This is the good news, the very heart of the gospel. Those who believe are saved to eternal life. Those who don't believe are destined to eternal separation from the God of all grace.

## Praise to the King!

Paul began this section with thanksgiving; now he closes it with praise. It is properly called a doxology which contains five parts: God as (1) King, (2) eternal, (3) immortal, (4) invisible, (5) the only wise God—the only God.

1. *God is King.* This is a figure of speech which indicates God's supreme sovereignty. When Jesus began His public ministry He came preaching the kingdom of God. God's kingdom is not just a territory (He reigns over everything); it is rulership in the hearts of men. All who accept Him crown Him King of their lives. They willingly submit in loving obedience to His royal reign.

2. *God is eternal.* "King eternal" is literally "King of the ages." This is the only place in all his writings that Paul uses this term. Very likely he had the Jewish concept of two ages in mind: the age that is, and the age to come. God is King of both, and also of all ages, as the phrase *for ever and ever* suggests. He is King of the ages —the God of the now and the God of the forever!

3. *God is immortal.* "Immortal" has the basic meaning of "not subject to death." All of us are subject to physical death, hence we are mortal. But God is immortal and incorruptible (the Greek word can mean either). This reminds us of a significant promise in 1 Corinthians 15:54. The God of immortality will lift those who were once subject to death and make them like unto himself. What a prospect! What a future! What a wonderful God!

4. *God is invisible.* The skeptic says, "Show me God and I'll believe in Him." The person of faith sees God not with the physical eye but with spiritual sight. Hebrews chapter 11 tells us Moses "endured, ... seeing him who is invisible." Colossians 1:15 says Christ is "the image of the invisible God." When we see Christ, we are seeing God, for Jesus told Philip, "He that hath seen me hath seen the Father" (John 14:9). Though God is invisible, that doesn't mean He cannot be seen. All it takes is the eye of faith.

5. *God is the only God.* In Paul's day polytheism (belief in many gods) was a big thing. Timothy was in

Ephesus, a city filled with corruption and idolatry. The church there was plagued with spiritual problems. Some gentile believers wanted to add Christianity to their collection of many gods. Paul declares that God is the only God—He alone is worthy of "honor and glory for ever and ever." This hasn't changed in 20 centuries: Our God is one God. He is worthy of praise!

**Fight the Good Fight!**

As Paul finishes his expression of thanksgiving with an "Amen," he moves back to his instructions to "son Timothy" with two military metaphors. He "charges" or commands Timothy to "war a good warfare." Later Paul uses a nautical term, *shipwreck*, in referring to two deserters of the faith.

What did Paul mean when he instructed Timothy to "war a good warfare"? In what sense is the Christian life a warfare? From what we've seen in this first chapter of 1 Timothy, the warfare was on at least two fronts: doctrinal and moral. The situation at Ephesus was critical. If the church was to advance, a fight against falsehood and sin must be waged. Timothy is like a lieutenant on the front lines while Paul is acting as a general in mapping strategies and relaying battle orders.

General Paul reminds Lieutenant Timothy of his original marching orders from the Commander in Chief: "the prophecies which went before on thee." This probably refers to Timothy's ordination into the ministry or his induction into missionary work. Paul will later mention this and include more detail. (See 4:14 and 2 Timothy 1:6.)

It is important for Timothy to remember who is really in charge. His call to warfare was given by God the Holy Spirit in prophetic utterances at the start of his ministry.

The same God that guided and helped him in missionary work and church problems, will now be with him as he faces false teachers, and the task of organizing the churches in Ephesus.

We need to remember that the Christian life is still a warfare. As soldiers we must be alert to infiltration by the enemy, and ready to do combat with the forces of evil. The attack can come from two quarters: from without or from within. Which is more dangerous would be hard to say. But if we can take a spiritual lesson from a physical reality, we would have to conclude that an army is more vulnerable to defeat when it has enemy agents within its ranks. Pogo, the lovable comic-strip possum, once said: "We have met the enemy, and he is us."

## A Good Conscience

In verse 19 Paul comes back to a pair he introduced in verse 5: faith and a good conscience. He says these are the offensive weapons in the "good fight." Notice how these two go together. It is impossible to hold to the faith if one is not careful to maintain a good conscience before God.

When Paul was making his defense in Jerusalem, he said, "Men and brethren, I have lived in all good conscience before God until this day" (Acts 23:1). When he said this, he was reviewing his whole life before he was converted as well as afterward. Even before he knew Christ, Paul had sought to keep a good conscience. So it is not enough for one to say he lives according to his conscience! Conscience needs to be instructed by the Word of God.

In 1 Timothy 1:19, 20, Paul goes on to say that some have rejected faith and a good conscience and have "shipwrecked" their faith. These people have turned away from the great truths of Christianity and are living in ways displeasing to God; they have given up a good conscience. They know what God's Word requires of them, but they go against their own consciences.

Think of the conscience as a rubber band. You pull it, and it snaps back. You pull it again, and it snaps back. But if you keep on pulling it, sooner or later it loses its elasticity, and finally does not snap back at all.

It is easy to lose the truth of God if we do not live in obedience to God's Word. We do not hold the truth simply in the mind; we learn it through the heart and the conscience, and we keep it by maintaining a good, pure conscience void of offense.

**Shipwrecked Faith**

Paul mentions two men, Hymeneus and Alexander, who have turned from the truth and are blaspheming God by their words and conduct. We don't know very much about these two. Hymeneus was a false teacher and is mentioned in 2 Timothy 2:17. Two Alexanders have connections with the city of Ephesus. One was a Jew (Acts 19:33, 34) and the other was a "coppersmith" who did a great deal of harm to Paul (see 2 Timothy 4:14). Perhaps the second Alexander is indicated here in 1 Timothy 1:20.

Strong language (and strong action) is seen in the clause "whom I have delivered unto Satan." How this was done we are not at all sure. Perhaps it followed the pattern set down by our Lord in Matthew 16:19. These two men may have been spiritually bound over to Satan as a disciplinary measure to teach them not to blaspheme. It probably means they were excommunicated from Christian fellowship as well.

This may seem drastic, but Hymeneus and Alexander were like a cancer. They could no longer be counseled and coddled; they must be cut off and removed. Verse 19 says they "put away" faith and a good conscience. *Put away* means "willfully rejected." Yet a glimmer of hope is seen in the final words of verse 20. This action by Paul is not only disciplinary, its hoped-for conclusion is remedial: "... that they may learn not to blaspheme." The purpose is to bring these two reprobates to the place of repentance.

As Paul rejoiced in God's mercy and overflowing grace, so this same grace is available to two men who have willfully turned their backs on God and become His enemies. There is hope, even for them, if they will repent and bow once again at the foot of the Cross—just as Saul of Tarsus did.

*Marvelous, infinite, matchless grace,*
*Freely bestowed on all who believe;*
*You that are longing to see His face,*
***Will you this moment His grace receive?***

Julia H. Johnston

CHAPTER **3**

# How to Act in Church

*Read 1 Timothy 2:1-15*

THE 4-YEAR-OLD KNELT ON THE FRONT SEAT of the car, his face pressed against the side window. Staring toward the house he half-sobbed, half-screamed his emotion-filled supplication: "Mommy! ... Mommy!" His mother had left him in the car so she wouldn't be bothered while she visited her friend "just for a minute." But the child, frightened and alone, didn't understand the concept of an adult "minute." He felt abandoned. So he kept up his desperate cry: "Mommy ... Mommy!"

Sometimes we may feel like this 4-year-old: alone, frightened, and doubtful if circumstances will return to normal. For the Christian, however, there is an antidote for these feelings. The child of God can pray and ask his Father to intervene in *any* circumstance. Prayer is the wonderful privilege of every believer. As we study the early verses of 1 Timothy 2, we will see some important principles that relate to prayer. And moving on into the chapter, we will begin to understand how each of us is to act during times of public worship.

### Prayer Comes First

"I exhort therefore, that, first of all, supplications, prayers, intercessions, and giving of thanks, be made for all men" (1 Timothy 2:1). Was Paul a stutterer? It sounds like he repeated himself. We might say he was redundant. But he really wasn't. He just used four different words that describe prayer.

Before we take a close look at the four words Paul used to describe prayer, notice his words *first of all.* These emphatically teach us that prayer is to be a priority item. Donald Guthrie says that "the words *first of all* relate not to primacy of time but primacy of importance" (*The Pastoral Epistles, Tyndale New Testament Commentaries* [Grand Rapids: Wm. B. Eerdmans Publishing Co., 1957], p. 69). In other words, we are to pray *first* before we complain to someone else; we are to pray *first* before we counsel someone else; we are to pray *first* before we condemn someone else for an error in judgment or a wrong action. In all things, we are to pray first!

Now let's look at the four words the Holy Spirit gave Paul as he exhorted Timothy (and the churches in Ephesus) regarding prayer.

1. *Supplication.* This word, *deesis,* has the basic meaning of request. It is not exclusively a religious word; it can mean a request made either to a fellowman or to God. But *deesis* connotes a sense of need. No one makes a request unless a sense of need is awakened.

2. *Prayer.* This word, *proseuche,* differs from the first. Supplication may be addressed either to man or God, but prayer is always and only addressed to God. There are certain needs that only God can satisfy.

3. *Intercession.* This word has the basic sense of petition. It is the noun form of the Greek verb *entugchano.* This word had acquired a special meaning in Paul's day: "to enter into a king's presence and to submit a petition to him."

This tells us a great deal about prayer. Believers have the right and privilege to bring their petitions to One who is King of kings and Lord of lords. Praying Christians can bring their needs, as well as those of others, to One who really cares and who really can do something for them.

4. *Giving of Thanks (Thanksgiving).* This word, *eucharistia*, brings in a beautiful balance. Prayer is not only asking God for things, it also means thanking God for who He is and what He does. We must not forget to give thanks. Too many of us view prayer as an exercise in complaining or an "I need" list, when it should be filled with thanksgiving.

So we have four kinds of prayer. Have you ever thought to ask yourself, "When was the last time I prayed according to Biblical standards? Furthermore, when did I pray *first* before thinking about a way out or acting on my own?"

## A Full Prayer List

Do you use a prayer list? Who is on it? Your family? pastor? relatives and friends? missionaries that you know or don't know? One little boy was overheard in his bedtime prayer. After listing all his family members and friends he added, "And God bless all the missionaries in the fields."

The Holy Spirit teaches us through this letter from Paul to Timothy that supplications, prayers, intercessions, and giving of thanks are to be made for everyone (v. 1), for kings, and for all that are in authority (v. 2). Since Paul lists everyone first it seems unnecessary to single out kings and those in positions of authority.

Remember, however, that Paul was in prison when he wrote this letter. "Kings" refers to emperors—and the one ruling at that time was Nero, a wicked and demented egotist. So the truth is underscored by Paul's exhortation: no matter how good or wicked a ruler or leader may be, Christians are to pray for him.

"All that are in authority" refers to all levels of government. In our society that includes city, county, state, and federal officials. When was the last time you prayed for them? The context of Paul's exhortation focuses on public worship. When did your church last pray for civil authorities?

## Why We Should Pray

Paul is very practical in his exhortation to prayer. He gives both the motivation and benefits in the closing clause of verse 2: "...that we may lead a quiet and peaceable life in all godliness and honesty." J.B. Phillips translates it this way: "So that our common life may be lived in peace and quiet, with a proper sense of God and of our responsibility to him for what we do with our lives." Commentators suggest that "honesty" is more accurately "holiness," or "reverence," since "honesty" meant more in 1611 than it does now.

Here are four reasons why we should pray for those in authority.

1. *Quietness.* The Greek adjective translated "quiet" occurs only here in the New Testament. W.E. Vine says the basic idea is that of "restfulness unmarred by disturbance."

2. *Peaceable Life (Peace-filled Life).* This is almost a synonym of the first term. Of it, Vine says *peaceable* "suggests the stillness that accompanied restfulness, in contrast to noisy commotion and merely bustling activity."

Marvin Vincent has suggested that the first term denotes a quietness arising from the absence of outside disturbance, and the second term speaks of tranquillity or peace that comes from within.

3. *Godliness.* The basic meaning here is piety or reverence. Godliness is God-likeness.

4. *Holiness.* The Greek word used here suggests the meanings of reverence, dignity, seriousness, respectfulness, and holiness. Certainly "honesty" is a part of holiness, but not all of it.

As you ponder these reasons for prayer, look at Phillip's paraphrase quoted on page 27. How closely does he capture the full meaning of these four words? Have you thought about why you pray in these terms? Do you feel that the circumstances of Paul's day make these principles applicable to that time only? Or are we dealing with timeless truths?

Finally, public (and private) prayer for all men and those in authority pleases God (v. 3). If this were the only motivation for prayer, it would be enough. God calls us to the ministry of prayer, and He is pleased when we respond.

### God's Plan—One Mediator

Beginning with the title in verse 3—"God our Saviour"—the emphasis shifts from the theme of prayer to that of salvation. This new theme extends through verse 7. Read these verses and feel the heartbeat of Paul as he writes of God's plan for the salvation of man.

The word *all* in verse 4 is the fifth time it has been used in this brief context. Does this verse say God will save all men? No, it says God *wants* to save all men. Salvation has been provided for all, but only those who accept it are saved. Being saved also means coming to a "knowledge of the truth." The "truth" here is the gospel, the revelation of God in Christ.

First Timothy 2:5 is one of the most significant verses in the whole Bible. It makes two exclusive declarations: (1) There is one God—no dualistic god of the Gnostics and no polytheistic god of the heathen is acceptable. The Scriptures teach there is but one God; He is Lord of the universe and the only Saviour. (2) There is "one mediator between God and men, the man Christ Jesus." A mediator is someone who stands between two parties and acts as a go-between. Note that Paul by the Spirit says "the *man* Christ Jesus." This reference to Christ reflects the deity and humanity of the Mediator. The One who dwelt with God in eternity came to dwell with man in time. Now He understands both sides. He reveals God to us and carries our needs to God. Truly He is an effective Mediator.

"Who gave himself a ransom for all" is another key truth of the gospel. The word *ransom* means "payment" and carries the full sense of "something that is given in exchange for another as the price of his redemption." In the first century the word was used for the ransom price paid to free a slave. The word *for* means "on behalf of." So Christ's ransom was on behalf of all people everywhere and for all time. But it is only effective for those who believe and accept that ransom as their own. That is why Paul adds, "to be testified (or "declared") in due time (at the appointed time)." The appointed time is "now"; today is the day of salvation. God still wants to save all men.

Paul's threefold ministry is described in verse 7. Some key words are found here. Why do you think he wrote what he did if this letter was to Timothy only? Didn't Timothy understand and accept Paul's ministry without question? This verse suggests that this letter was to have a wider audience than just one "son in the faith." The churches in Ephesus must recognize the authority Paul has when he makes such declarations as he has just done. They must accept as divine truth the fact that Christ is the only Saviour, the only Mediator, and the only One able to pay the ransom for sin.

## Pentecostal Praying

"I will therefore that men pray everywhere, lifting up holy hands, without wrath and doubting" (1 Timothy 2:8). This is a transitional verse. That is, it refers back to the first verse and becomes a bridge to the next verse. Earlier Paul wrote about the what, who, and why of prayer; now he gives instructions regarding the how. Lifting up one's hands in prayer is very Biblical (see 1 Kings 8:22; Psalms 141:2 and 143:6). It shows earnest desire and is a picture of surrender. It can also be an act of faith such as reaching out to receive a gift. Remember, too, that Paul is giving instructions concerning public worship. So the uplifted hands are expected to be seen in church.

These hands are to be holy (devout, morally pure). God expects the one who prays to back up his prayers with a holy life. Paul may have been thinking of Jesus' words in the Sermon on the Mount when he added the next phrase "without wrath." Jesus taught that God won't accept our gift at the altar if we harbor a grudge against a brother (Matthew 5:23, 24). He also said we must forgive if we want forgiveness (Matthew 6:15).

"Doubting" can include the meaning of disputing and dissension. All of these are hindrances to prayer. The antidote for doubt is faith. John penned these wonderful words of assurance by the Spirit: "This is the confidence that we have in him, that, if we ask any thing according to his will, he heareth us" (1 John 5:14). We ought to come into God's presence with uplifted hands and pray everywhere (v. 8) for everyone (v. 1).

## How Women Are to Dress

Perhaps some might say, "Now Paul has quit preaching and gone to meddling!" After telling the men how to pray, Paul instructs the women on how to dress. But the modern reader must remember that Paul is writing from a specific historical context. Also, he is thinking in terms of public worship concerning how men and women are to act in church.

A careful reading of verses 9 and 10 shows three negatives and three positives concerning dress. Let's consider the negatives first. They are (1) braided hair, (2) gold and pearls, (3) expensive clothes. All three of these relate to first-century customs. Some women spent hours preparing their long hair in highly fashionable styles, fastening their plaits with ribbons and brightly colored bows. Rich women would interweave gold, silver, and pearls in their hairstyles, causing them to sparkle. It is very likely that the expensive clothes were outlandish in style and color, drawing undue attention to the wearer.

All this fashionable adornment would be (and probably was) distracting in the public worship service. In an Ephesian church with several wealthy Christians, the services might look like an "Easter Parade" to us.

So Paul instructs his readers about adornment that is "appropriate for women who profess to worship God" (v. 10, *New International Version*). The three positives are (1) modest apparel, (2) decency, (3) sobriety. Paul didn't get into an argument regarding the length of the skirt or the wearing of slacks (those weren't the issues in the first century), he merely laid down three principles: (1) modesty, (2) decency, and (3) propriety or good judgment.

Immodest or inappropriate dress distracts from the

witness of a Christian woman. It brings attention to her instead of the Lord. It may distract others from seeing her "good works" (v. 10) which are to be the true adornment of those who profess godliness.

As we consider the question of women's dress, we must go beyond this one passage to determine the Biblical teaching and our response. But Paul gives us all a good starting point in the guidelines of modesty, decency, and propriety.

## Must Women Be Silent?

After writing about a woman's appearance in public he turns the coin over and informs Timothy about a woman's place in the church (vv. 11, 12). As with the subject of dress, this teaching reflects the culture and situation of the first century.

Women occupied a low position in Jewish society. They were not people, they were things, entirely at the disposal of their fathers or husbands. Women were forbidden to learn the Law. They had no active part in the synagogue services but were confined to a separate section in the gallery. A man came to the synagogue to *learn*, but a woman, if allowed to come, came only to *listen*. Women were forbidden to teach in a school, and did not even teach their own small children at home.

Women, slaves, and children were classed together. In the Jewish morning prayer a man thanked God that he was not "a gentile, a slave, or a woman." We in the 20th century must accept this cultural view of women as the backdrop for Paul's instructions regarding a woman's place in the church. (Compare his teaching in 1 Corinthians 14:33-35.)

Because the women were uneducated, they were to "learn in silence." They were to be submissive and not usurp the authority given to men. They were not to teach. Functions such as teaching and governing in the church should be performed by men because (1) Adam preceded Eve (having priority by virtue of creation and experience, v. 13), and (2) Eve was deceived—not Adam (v. 14). She sinned because she succumbed to Satan's deception.

Christianity has elevated women to a social status equal with men. The way we interpret these instructions in our day and culture is significantly different from how the church observed them in Paul's day.

The apostle concludes his teaching about women on a positive note. He says they are to continue in faith, love, and holiness with sobriety. If they do this, their public witness will please and honor God.

CHAPTER **4**

# Qualifications for Leaders

*Read 1 Timothy 3:1-16*

"I WILL BE A SERVANT OF THE PEOPLE, not a bureaucrat of big government," the candidate declares during the campaign. But in reality he is seeking power and prestige for himself, not servanthood. "I want only to serve—nothing else" is the claim made at the election victory celebration. But later we see that the politician doesn't refuse the bimonthly salary or the generous expense account and fringe benefits that come with the office.

It seems the world's idea of service is not that of Christ who said, "I am among you as he that serveth" (Luke 22:27). On one occasion when James and John voiced political ambition, Jesus rebuked all His disciples by saying:

> Ye know that they which are accounted to rule over the gentiles exercise lordship over them; and their great ones exercise authority upon them. But so shall it not be among you: but whosoever will be great among you, shall be your minister: and whosoever of you will be the chiefest, shall be servant of all (Mark 10:42-44).

In our study of 1 Timothy 3 we will encounter the words *minister* and *servant*. Although this chapter is titled "Qualifications for Leaders," it could very well be subtitled "What Does It Mean to Serve?" As we study

Paul's instructions to Timothy, we must keep Jesus' words about service in sharp focus. Servanthood in the kingdom of God is very different from the kind of "service" we see performed by members of a secular society.

## The Office of "Bishop"

When we in the 20th century read the term *bishop* we immediately form a mental image of a high-ranking member of an ecclesiastical hierarchy. But it was not so in the first century. A bishop was an overseer or spiritual minister and teacher of a local church. *Pastor, bishop,* and *elder* are interchangeable terms. Acts 20:17 and 28 use three Greek words that show these to be synonymous. In none of the New Testament references to pastor, bishop, and elder is there any suggestion of rank; they are all on the same level.

Paul introduces the qualifications of pastors by the phrase "This is a true saying." We have seen this earlier (1:15) and will see it again. This phrase is a structural key to Paul's letters to Timothy. Paul is about to embark on an important matter. "If a man desire the office of a bishop, he desireth a good work."

The verses that follow list 15 qualifications for the spiritual leader. Ten are positive and five are negative. A 16th in the list addresses the pastor's reputation as it relates to the world. As we consider each of these 16, think of the practical application beyond the primary reference pastor. Most of these qualities are to be seen in the life of every believer.

## Character Counts Big

The spiritual leader must be:
 1. *Blameless*. This seems to be an overriding

characteristic. Literally it means "not to be laid hold of." Other translations are "above reproach" and "without fault." The Greek word is used in 6:14 and is translated "unrebukable." The Christian's life and testimony must be so clean that no one can find any fault.

2. *The husband of one wife.* This moral qualification reflects the social and cultural situation of the first century. Polygamy and easy divorce and remarriage surrounded the church. Paul, under the inspiration of the Spirit, says monogamy—one wife at one time—is to be the requirement for pastors. The spiritual leader is to be a "one-wife man." He must not remarry if he has a living spouse. He must be faithful to his wife and give her all the love and devotion she deserves. Marital entanglements beyond the "one" can bring discredit to his position as a spiritual leader and reproach on the church.

3. *Vigilant.* Vigilance is a mental qualification that is required of everyone (1 Peter 5:8), but especially of pastors because they are given responsibility over the church (Hebrews 13:17).

4. *Sober.* The meaning here is "temperate." A sober person is one who does not become intoxicated by alcohol. But *temperate* had a broader meaning. Richard L. Dresselhaus says:

> The Greek word ... means "free from excess, passion, ruckus, confusion, etc., ... well-balanced, self-controlled." A spiritual leader is well-oriented mentally, socially, spiritually, and physically (*The Deacon and His Ministry* [Springfield, MO: Gospel Publishing House, 1977], p. 23).

5. *Of good behavior.* The basic meaning here is "orderly," "respectable," "honorable." It could have application to the leader's manner of dress, the

orderliness of his office, even whether his grass was cut! (or whatever made his residence of the first-century look respectable).

6. *Given to hospitality.* The word from which this is taken literally means "loving strangers." Christian hospitality was one of the important virtues of the Early Church. It is still a command to Christians everywhere — and especially to those who would set the example as spiritual leaders.

7. *Apt to teach* or "able to teach." W.E. Vine makes this helpful comment: "Not merely a readiness to teach is implied, but the spiritual power to do so as the outcome of prayerful meditation in the Word of God and the practical application of its truth to oneself" (page 51). Every pastor is first of all a teacher (see Ephesians 4:11).

**Negatives to Avoid**

8. *Not given to wine.* It must be recognized that total abstinence was not the practice in the first century church. The word used by Paul meant to "overdrink" or to be "addicted" to wine. The spiritual leader was not to overindulge in the only safe drink available to him. He must be aware of the Bible's warnings against strong drink and drunkenness in such passages as Proverbs 23:19-21, 29-35. Alcohol dulls the senses and drunkenness brings public disgust.

9. *No striker.* This had nothing to do with labor strikes or walkouts. It means the spiritual leader is a nonviolent individual. Very possibly this connects with *not given to wine.* When someone becomes drunk he usually becomes loud and abusive. This often results in a fight. Such behavior is completely out of character for *any* Christian, and especially a spiritual leader.

10. *Not greedy of filthy lucre.* The *New International*

*Version* translates this "not a lover of money." J.B. Phillips says it this way: "He must not be ... greedy for money." There is no inherent evil in money, it is a person's greed that makes it "filthy." Paul addresses this point in 1 Timothy 6:10.

11. *Patient.* This is the only positive quality in this verse with five negatives. Note that it is placed in the middle. Its basic meaning is "gentle": the spiritual leader is to be patient and gentle. When the pressures mount, that's when gentleness must reign supreme.

12. *Not a brawler.* The literal meaning is "abstinence from fighting." It is the task of the spiritual leader to be a peacemaker, not a fighter. In our day of "causes" the Christian must remember this injunction: "not violent but gentle, not quarrelsome" (v. 3, *New International Version*). "Keep cool" is sound advice.

13. *Not covetous.* Covetousness was denounced by God at the giving of the Ten Commandments. Jesus didn't give it any extra credits in His teaching about the Kingdom. All the New Testament writers denounce it. Every Christian should avoid it like the plague.

## Ruling the Family

Verses 4 and 5 deal with the family relationships of the spiritual leader. He is to be:

14. *One that ruleth well his own house.* The Bible always views the father as the head of the marriage and the family. He is to provide leadership, protection, and care. His provision is to be both spiritual and material. So it is understandable that Paul would make this qualification part of the pastor's requirements. The apostle also adds a parenthetical statement that argues the point beyond any contradiction: "If anyone does not know how to manage his own family, how can he take

care of God's church?" (v. 5, *New International Version*). This is a very sobering thought.

## A Good Reputation

15. *Not a novice.* Leadership requires experience and wisdom for making decisions. The new convert or inexperienced Christian faces many pitfalls that lessen his chances of making the right decisions. The Greek word here is the root of our word *neophyte*. Paul goes on to give two reasons: "lest being lifted up with pride," and "he fall into the condemnation of the devil." The first is quite clear. We might paraphrase it this way: "In case he becomes inflated with a sense of his own importance."

The second reason is not quite so clear. Three possible explanations exist: (1) The devil rebelled against God and was cast from heaven because of pride—hence this is a warning against pride. (2) The new convert may allow pride to come in and thus give the devil a chance to bring a charge against him or the church. (3) The word *diabolos* also means "slanderer." The neophyte's unworthy conduct or unwise decisions may be cause for slander. However we take it, the conceited spiritual leader is a liability to the church.

16. *He has a "good report of them which are without."* Here the overriding qualification is a good reputation in the world beyond the doors of the church. The spiritual leader must have the respect and confidence of community leaders and business people. This does not mean he must compromise his convictions. It does mean he must pay his bills, support worthy community projects and be an all-around good citizen. This is a requirement of all believers, not just pastors.

## Deacons Are Like Waiters

Acts 6 tells us the first deacons were selected to "serve

tables" (v. 2). This was a unique situation caused by rapid growth in the Early Church, and the need for men who could oversee the daily distribution of food. The deacon's function expanded beyond that beginning point of waiting on tables to other forms of service.

*Deacon, servant,* and *minister* all come from the Greek word *diakonos.* Although Paul does not list the functions of the office of deacon in verses 8 through 13, he does give the qualifications. Most are identical to those listed in the previous paragraph. Let's consider those not already covered.

1. *A deacon must be "grave."* This doesn't mean "sourpuss." Its basic meaning is "serious" or "worthy of honor and respect." He recognizes the seriousness of God's work and takes full responsibility for the duties to be performed. This brings him respect from others.

2. *A deacon is not to be "double-tongued."* He doesn't engage in double-talk—saying one thing to one person and something else to another. He is truthful and sincere. His word is trustworthy.

3. *A deacon holds "the mystery of the faith in a pure conscience."* In the New Testament, *mystery* referred to a secret unknown to the masses but revealed to the believer in Christ. Connected with *faith* it means the truths of the gospel revealed in Jesus Christ. The deacon, knowing the tenets of faith (the truth found in the gospel), will hold these with a pure and clear conscience.

4. *A deacon must be "proved" and "found blameless."* G. Raymond Carlson explains verse 10 this way:

> The Bible warns against choosing men for the office of deacon too hastily. A man must prove himself, develop maturity, and give evidence of the qualities the Scriptures delineate before he is considered for the office (*And He*

*Gave Pastors* [Springfield, MO: Gospel Publishing House, 1979], p. 490).

## Wives or Deaconesses?

Because the Greek word *gyne* is used for "women" and "wife" some have questioned whether Paul was writing about the wives of deacons or the office of deaconess in verse 11. Because the context (both before and after) focuses on deacons, most translators and commentators go with "wives."

Four qualifications for deacons' wives are given. Two repeat those given to deacons: the wives are to be grave (serious) and sober (temperate). The other two qualifications involve discretion, self-control, and industry.

1. *Not slanderers.* Some might say that Paul would get to gossip and women sooner or later. But the first-century culture was conducive to gossip. Women would gather at the well or market and exchange family news. Paul wants Christian women (and men) to know that God doesn't approve of slanderers (called "malicious talkers" in the *New International Version*). Discretion on the part of women married to leaders in the church is very important. Self-control will keep gossip in check. Gossip, out of control, can turn to slander.

2. *Faithful in all things.* Moffatt translates this "absolutely trustworthy." The Christian woman must set an example of industry and faithfulness. This honors God and gives an effective witness within and without the church.

Verse 13 ends Paul's instructions regarding deacons. It commends those who serve well. They gain the esteem and respect of those whom they serve and find boldness (assurance) in their relationship with Jesus Christ. So the rewards of faithful service are both horizontal and vertical.

## The Mystery of Godliness

In the final paragraph of this chapter (vv. 14-16) Paul gives us the keynote of the entire letter. This is a key passage: it tells us Paul's purpose for writing and gives us a creed-like statement that summarizes the gospel.

Paul was hoping to visit Timothy soon. But because he might be delayed, he was writing to Timothy so he might know "how thou oughtest to behave thyself in the house of God." Was Timothy misbehaving in church? No. What Paul was saying didn't have to do with Timothy's behavior so much as it did with his official duties among the churches in Ephesus. Those duties are spelled out in the entire letter.

The second half of verse 15 introduces two doctrinal definitions: one on the church and the other on the gospel. Note that the "church" is called the "house [household] of God." This is a clear reference to the body of Christian believers rather than a physical building.

Verse 16 is the zenith of this letter. Coming halfway through the Epistle, it highlights the life and ministry of Jesus. Many see this as a creedal hymn used by the early Christians. "Without controversy great is the mystery of godliness" is found nowhere else in the New Testament. It forms a bridge between the practical instructions given earlier and the doctrinal truth of the gospel that follows.

The six-line stanza could profitably be committed to memory. The first three statements are understood only by divine revelation—hence the "great mystery." The last three are attested by historical records in the Gospels and Acts. They are not in chronological order but possibly in order of importance.

God was manifest in the flesh,
justified in the Spirit,
seen of angels,
preached unto the gentiles,
believed on in the world,
received up into glory.

Praise God for the coming of His Son and the privilege we have of spreading the good news!

CHAPTER **5**

# How to Deal With False Doctrine

*Read 1 Timothy 4:1-16*

WHY DO WE NEED MEDICAL DOCTORS? Since God has created us and knows all about us, He can help us recover from sickness or cure us of disease. Medical science has shown that God has endowed living beings with innate healing properties. Doctors don't heal; God heals through the natural processes He has created within us or through supernatural intervention as the result of believing prayer.

But doctors play a part in the overall healing process. God has allowed medical science to discover natural laws that relate to the human body so that doctors can help suffering people. By diagnosing what is wrong and prescribing certain remedies, doctors work with the laws of nature to produce a conducive environment for healing.

When we study the word *doctrine,* it is interesting to note that one meaning 700 years ago was "what the doctor teaches." As we read 1 Timothy 4 we find the word *doctrine* used four times. It's a key word. Paul wrote to Timothy and it seems the apostle filled the role of a spiritual doctor. He diagnosed the disease, then prescribed the remedy. His prescription formula might read something like this: "Destroy the disease of false doctrine with a big dose of sound doctrine."

## False Teachers Are Losers

"Now the Spirit speaketh expressly, that in the latter times some shall depart from the faith...." Paul refers to the Holy Spirit only twice in this first letter to Timothy. It is noteworthy that the verses using *Spirit* are back to back. Here in 4:1 it is the Spirit speaking clearly about apostasy in the "latter times."

What is apostasy? And who is an apostate? *Apostasy* is "renunciation, abandonment, defection, departure, withdrawal," and "a falling away." An apostate is someone who does these things with regard to his religious beliefs. The Biblical statement is very accurate: "some shall depart from the faith." This means they willfully abandon the belief that Jesus is the Christ, the Son of God. What they *do* believe after this act of apostasy is incredible: "seducing spirits and doctrines of demons."

An apostate is a loser. He has left the grace and love of the Father to pursue a course that leads to hell. He has abandoned the truth that brings life to follow the falsehood that ends in death. He is a loser and has joined company with hypocritical liars and those whose consciences are "seared with a hot iron."

The language used by Paul here shows this apostasy to be a willful, deliberate act. Those who abandoned the faith knew better. They weren't deceived or tricked; they deliberately withdrew from their position in God by a willful choice. Now that they had made that choice, they completed their defection by adopting new beliefs that branded their consciences with a red-hot iron. Their zeal was now turned to teaching false doctrine.

## Asceticism Won't Make You Holy

Two of their false teachings are given in verse 3: "They

forbid people to marry and order them to abstain from certain foods" (*New International Version*). This asceticism reflected the early evidence of Gnosticism. The Gnostics taught that all matter is evil and only that which is spirit is good. One's abstinence from marriage and meat, they said, would make him holy and acceptable to God.

Paul doesn't refute the first teaching here, but he does the second. Regarding matter as evil, what are we to do with Genesis 1:31: "God saw every thing that he had made, and, behold, it was very good"? Regarding marriage, God brought Adam a wife and said: "It is not good that man should be alone" (Genesis 2:18). Jesus gave His sanction to marriage when He attended a wedding feast in Cana (John 2:1-11). Nowhere does the Bible say marriage is evil. If a person remains celibate it is to be his choice, not obedience to a taboo taught by others.

Regarding abstinence from certain foods, Paul repeats a principle given elsewhere in Scripture: God has created all food for our consumption. Before the Flood, man may have been a vegetarian. But God told Noah that animals could be eaten as food, as well as vegetables and grains (Genesis 9:3). In Romans Paul points out that the "weak in the faith" avoid eating meat and restrict themselves to a vegetable diet (Romans 14:1, 2). He says that this is not necessary for everyone. Then he gives the overriding principle: "He that eateth, eateth to the Lord, for he giveth God thanks; and he that eateth not, to the Lord he eateth not, and giveth God thanks" (Romans 14:6).

This is the emphasis of verses 4 and 5: "Every creature of God is good, and nothing [is] to be refused, it if be received with thanksgiving: for it is sanctified [consecrated] by the word of God and prayer." Saying grace at the table is an act of worship. It provides an opportunity to thank God for His provision and to ask Him to make the food "holy." (That's the primary meaning of *sanctify:* to set apart as a holy thing.)

## The Remedy: Sound Doctrine

The antidote for asceticism is knowing and believing the truth (v. 3) which is good or sound doctrine (v. 6). The first five verses spell out the problem, now verses 6-16 give the solution. Paul by the Spirit gives very practical advice to Timothy. Here he provides the details of his prescription formula: "Destroy the disease of false doctrine with a big dose of sound doctrine!"

"You will be a faithful minister of Christ Jesus if you remind your church members of these things. You will show yourself as a man nourished by the message of the true faith and by the sound teaching he has followed" (v. 6, *Phillips*). Timothy's earliest training was in Judaism. But as a young person he was converted to Christianity. He personally gained his spiritual strength and stature from the truths he absorbed and the sound teaching or doctrine he followed. These are to be the starting point of his ministry toward others.

How important it is that we gain spiritual knowledge and strength before we attempt to teach or help others. Soundness of doctrine is an absolute necessity for a ministry that honors the Lord and lifts others.

## Flex Your Spiritual Muscles

Verse 7 gives a negative and a positive. First, Timothy is to "refuse profane and old wives' fables." *Profane* was used in chapter 1, verse 9, when Paul was listing various types of sinners. Here in 4:7 it serves as an adjective to modify the word *fables*. Almost everything in Ephesus was profane. Timothy, as a spiritual leader, was to refuse or reject godless myths.

The "old wives' fables" were tales which old women might tell to children. They are imaginary ideas or made-up stories that have no basis in truth. These could become side issues that lead away from the central truth of the gospel. The "good minister of Jesus Christ" (v. 6) must refuse to get sidetracked by godless myths and old wives' tales.

What he should do is flex his spiritual muscles. As the Bible puts it: "Exercise thyself ... unto godliness. For bodily exercise profiteth little [is of some value]: but godliness is profitable unto all things" (vv. 7, 8). Paul was prompted by the Spirit to use the figure of athletics in several of the letters he penned (see 1 Corinthians 9:24; Philippians 3:14; 2 Timothy 4: 7, 8). Some have misread Paul's statement here. He did not say that physical exercise is unprofitable. He said it is of some profit or value. But he uses physical exercise as the backdrop to contrast the greater truths of spiritual exercise.

What is spiritual exercise? Is it not those thoughts, words, and actions that result in godliness? And "godliness is profitable unto all things, having promise of the life that now is, and of that which is to come" (v. 8). So we see the contrast: physical exercise has profit for this life, but godliness is profitable for this life and the next. The wise person will train himself to be godly. This kind of training develops not only the body but the mind and spirit as well.

## Hope in the Living God

Next, we have another "faithful saying" (v. 9). But here we discover a puzzle. Does verse 9 go with verse 8 or verse 10? Commentators are divided because the Greek construction can be understood either way.

In verse 10 Paul writes that he was giving the ministry all he had. One of the verbs he uses is the Greek word *agonizo* from which we get our word *agonize*. Just as a runner exerts what seems to be his last ounce of energy to cross the finish line first, so Paul was striving with all his might in the ministry given to him by God.

This was not bragging on Paul's part. His motivation was a strong trust (or "hope") in God. This fits so well with the last part of verse 8. If Paul was exercising himself toward godliness as he was encouraging Timothy to do, that godly life-style had "promise of the life that now is, and of that which is to come." It also proved that Paul's hope was in "the living God, who is the Saviour [Preserver] of all men, [and] specially of those that believe."

### Set an Example for Others

Beginning with verse 11 Paul gives Timothy practical advice concerning his public ministry. Perhaps it will help if Paul's counsel is put in list form. Notice 10 rules of practical instruction.

1. Command these things.
2. Teach these things.
3. Don't let anyone look down on you because you are young.
4. Set an example for the believers:
   a. In speech,
   b. In life,
   c. In love,
   d. In faith,
   e. In purity.
5. Devote yourself:

      a. To the public reading of Scripture,
      b. To preaching,
      c. To teaching.
  6. Do not neglect your gift, which was given you through a prophetic message when the elders laid their hands on you.
  7. Be diligent in these matters.
  8. Give yourself wholly to them, so that everyone may see your progress.
  9. Watch your life and doctrine closely.
  10. Persevere in them, because if you do, you will save both yourself and your hearers (vv. 11-16, *New International Version*).

As you read these 10, did you ask yourself: "Does that apply to me?" Certain ones in the list apply only to Timothy in his unique situation. Others have broader application. How about number 3? Timothy was perhaps 30 when Paul wrote to him. Even 30-year-old people may be looked down on by others. Do you fit that category? Does Paul's advice apply to you?

Number 4 gives a principle that is applicable to everyone—no matter what his or her age. Paul's advice to Timothy—silence criticism by worthy conduct—is a universal truth. If we are faithful to set a godly example in these five areas, God will be pleased with us.

### Discipline Yourself

It seems the first six in the list have to do with Timothy's public ministry while the last four relate to his personal conduct. Timothy is to be diligent, consistent, watchful, and persistent. This takes self-discipline.

Verse 16 is a key verse; it contains the truths of 9 and 10 above. "Life" and "doctrine" are two sides of a coin. A person cannot say he believes something without proving it by his life. By the same token, a person's life must reflect his "doctrine" or set of beliefs. The Greek for this clause is literally: "Give attention to yourself and to the teaching." A person must watch his own life, not just his outward actions, but also his inner thoughts and feelings. No matter how "correct" his doctrine may be, if there is a flaw in his life, his "ministry" is ruined.

If Timothy does all these things he will save himself and his hearers. This is not a salvation by works. What Paul is writing here reflects Philippians 2:12: "Work out your own salvation with fear and trembling." God does the initial work of saving us, but we must be diligent, consistent, watchful, and persistent to continue in that salvation. Our Christian life-style and sound doctrine will then be a double-barreled force against false doctrine.

## Truth or Error?

Recognizing false doctrine in our day is not an easy task. Very often it is disguised as spiritual half-truths or new "revelations." Because they sound like the Bible and are propagated by those who appear very religious, it is difficult to determine their validity. But there are several ways to test any teaching to find out whether it is counterfeit or not.

The first and greatest test is, "Does it agree with the teachings of the Bible?" The person who shares his new revelation with you may quote any number of Scripture verses to support his doctrine. But look those references up and study them in their contexts. Do they really mean what that person said they mean? If the doctrine is false you will discover that Scripture has been twisted and made to mean something never intended when the Holy Spirit first gave it.

Second, seek counsel from your pastor, a spiritual

leader in the church, or Christians who have shown stability and maturity. Talk frankly about the issue and your feelings. Ask them to study pertinent Bible passages with you. Seek truth together. And pray together for the Spirit's illumination.

Third, don't be swayed by your emotions. Truth is not based on subjective feelings. Truth is an absolute and finds its source and expression in God's Word. Pray for the wisdom to hold steady during a crisis period when your mind may dictate one thing and your heart another.

CHAPTER **6**

# How to Treat Others

*Read 1 Timothy 5:1 to 6:2*

IN THIS FIRST LETTER TO TIMOTHY, Paul has given some heavy warnings and instructions. Much of Paul's counsel in the first four chapters related to doctrine and church administration. As the Holy Spirit prompted Paul to continue this letter, Paul now focused attention on relationships. Because we live in society instead of seclusion, we must be aware of others and treat them in a way that shows respect and concern. How we treat others also shows the depth and effectiveness of our Christianity.

Paul addressed the relationships that Timothy faced in overseeing the churches in Ephesus. Those relationships primarily focused on widows (vv. 3-16), elders (v. 17-25), and servants and masters (6:1, 2). But the counsel given Timothy is so practical and universal that it has great relevance for our day as well. So our task in this chapter will be to understand the text of 1 Timothy 5:1 through 6:2: first, as it applies to Timothy in the first century; and, second, as the timeless principles apply to us in the 20th century. If you haven't already done so, stop for 3 minutes right now and read the passage.

### Members of the Congregation

"Rebuke not an elder, but entreat him as a father; and

the younger men as brethren; the elder women as mothers; the younger as sisters, with all purity." Paul begins by writing about age relationships. The word *elder* here does not refer to church officials of that name but to older men in the congregation. So Timothy is told how to relate to those older and younger than himself.

If an older man needs rebuke, Timothy is to do it with gentleness and kindness, as if he were his father. He is to treat older women as he would his mother, younger men as he would a brother, and younger women as he would a sister. These instructions show a spirit of family relationship within the congregation. An added caution is to be observed with younger women; Timothy is to treat them as "sisters, with all purity." As a spiritual leader Timothy's relationship with women is to be above reproach.

Perhaps this is one verse that prompted the use of "Brother" and "Sister" as terms of address in the church. (For one of the first, see Acts 9:17.) These expressions show a close relationship: those who are born again are members of the family of God. They are all different but because of spiritual rebirth, they are now brothers and sisters in the Lord. And, as such, they are to show mutual respect and express the Christian love the Holy Spirit has put in their hearts. Their relationships are to reflect the work of grace in their lives.

## Widows in Need

Social security benefits were nonexistent in the first century. Widowhood could be a very trying experience. Because women were uneducated and fulfilled primarily domestic roles, the loss of a husband often left a widow destitute. In the Jewish community widows were cared for as part of the synagogue's benevolence services. The church followed this custom too (Acts 6).

In Paul's instructions in verses 3-16 we see at least four classes of widows. First, there are real widows (called "widows indeed" in the King James Version). Second, there are widows with relatives able to support them. Third, Paul refers to widows living in pleasure. And fourth, there are young widows. All were in need, but some were in greater need than others.

The "real widow" (identified as the one "who is left all alone" in the *New International Version* text of vv. 3 and 5) was the most destitute and desolate. She had no children and no relatives. So the church is to be her family. She is to be given "honor" (proper recognition, value, reverence). This "honor" may include compensation and care as Goodspeed suggests in his translation of verse 3: "Look after widows who are really dependent."

Verse 5 gives the characteristics of a true Christian widow. She trusts (puts her hope) in God and prays continually night and day, asking God for help. Though she is desolate she maintains a strong faith in God as her Provider. The Lord becomes a "husband" to the Christian widow who trusts and prays.

The second class of widows is those with relatives able to support them. These are described in verses 4, 8, and 16. *The Amplified Bible* (v. 4) clearly shows how this class of widow is to be treated:

> If a widow has children or grandchildren, see to it that these are first made to understand that it is their religious duty (to defray their natural obligation to those) at home, and make return to their parents or grandparents [for all their care by contributing to their maintenance], for this is acceptable in the sight of God.

Both Jews and Christians were very conscious of the responsibility required by the Fifth Commandment. But Paul, moved by the Holy Spirit, adds an even heavier responsibility: "If any provide not for his own, and specially for those of his own house, he hath *denied the faith, and is worse than an infidel*!" (v. 8, emphasis added).

We live in an age when family responsibilities can be easily shifted to the State. Grown children of elderly parents can demand public charity when their personal irresponsibility and selfishness foster neglect. But those in the church must be different. The care of elderly parents is a witness of true religion and becomes an expression of genuine love and gratefulness by the children.

The third class of widows Paul mentions is those living in pleasure (vv. 6 and 7). In the Ephesian culture and elsewhere in the first century, many single women resorted to immoral living as a means of support. Paul may have had this in mind when he said, "But she that liveth in pleasure is dead while she liveth."

## Qualifications for Widow Support

Having clearly defined who a real widow is, Paul now gives instructions regarding the church's relationship to her. Because she is destitute and in need of care, she is eligible to be put on an official list of widows. But there are certain qualifications beyond need. Verses 9 and 10 give them.

1. She must be over 60 years old. Some commentators feel this qualification suggests an "Order of Widows" who were godly widows over 60 set apart for special tasks. Their duties are given in the verse that follows. We know there was such an order in the third century but we

cannot be sure one existed in A.D. 64 when Paul wrote this letter. Because he writes about younger widows in verses 11-16, it may be simply that widows above 60 were eligible for full support of the church if they had no other means.

2. She must have been a faithful wife. *The wife of one man* literally means a "one-man wife." It does not have to mean "married only once." The main idea is monogamous fidelity.

3. She must be well known for her good deeds. Reputation is very important. As someone has said, "Character is what we are but reputation is what others report about our character." These good works are then listed in a priority order: (1) bringing up children, (2) showing hospitality, (3) washing the saints' feet, (4) relieving the afflicted, and (5) doing all kinds of other good works. Is there anything else? These are certainly high qualifications!

## Counsel for Younger Widows

At verse 11 Paul begins to address the fourth class of widows. It seems he has some very harsh things to say to them. Stop and reread verses 11-15 from one or two different translations to get the thrust of Paul's instructions. He makes several points:

1. Younger widows will be tempted by their sexual desire and will want to remarry—so they are not to be put on the widows' list.

2. Younger widows will lack the spiritual maturity to devote themselves to prayer and good works—requirements given in verses 5 and 10—and will leave their first pledge of devotion to Christ.

3. Younger widows will become idle busybodies,

"speaking things they ought not." Being idle, they may go from house to house picking up and spreading private information. A *busybody* is one who pays attention to things that do not concern him or her; he is meddlesome.

4. Younger widows should remarry and take the responsibility of a home and family. This will stop Satan from bringing reproach on the church and the Christian community.

Sobering counsel. Yet when considered carefully in light of the first-century culture, it is very sensible and helpful. What younger widows in our day face may be slightly different. But the counsel is not out of date or irrelevant.

Before moving on to a new set of relationships, Paul summarizes his counsel concerning widows in verse 16. J.B. Phillips paraphrases it this way: "As a general rule it should be taken for granted that any Christians who have widows in the family circle should do everything possible for them and not allow them to become the church's responsibility. The church will then be free to look after those widows who are alone in the world."

## How to Treat Elders

Spiritual leaders are the second major group Paul's practical instructions cover. He deals with several items: how much a pastor should be paid, how he should be protected from slander, how he should be rebuked publicly if he has sinned. These instructions are found in verses 17-20. Additional counsel is given in verses 21-25, but we will consider that under the next heading.

First, "Let the elders that rule well be counted worthy of double honor, especially they who labor in the word and doctrine" (v. 17). Paul has pastors in view here since *rule* means "superintend." The *New International Ver-*

*sion* calls them "the elders who direct the affairs of the church." These men are worthy of "double honor." No doubt this refers to remuneration, especially in the context of verse 18 where Paul quotes two passages of Scripture: Deuteronomy 25:4 and Luke 10:7. *Double* may not mean "twice" in the strictest sense. "Ample" or "generous" is probably closer to the intent of Paul's words. Special consideration is to be given those who preach and teach the Word.

Second, "Against an elder receive not an accusation, but before two or three witnesses" (v. 19). It was Jewish law that said no man was to be condemned on the evidence of a single witness. Jesus taught this principle when He told us how to treat a brother who sins against us (Matthew 18:16). Now Paul, under the inspiration of the Spirit, applies this principle to the polity of the church. It would protect spiritual leaders from unwarranted slander.

Third, "Them that sin rebuke before all, that others also may fear" (v. 20). If a spiritual leader is guilty of sin, he is to be rebuked publicly. Whether this is before the whole church or just the body of elders is not clear. But the reason for this public rebuke is plain: it will deter others from falling into the same sin.

These instructions have direct reference to spiritual leaders. It would be improper to apply them to Christians in general (with the exception of the second; see Matthew 18:16). But they are important words because they tell us how we are to treat those whom God has put over us as spiritual leaders.

## A Charge to Timothy

Although verses 21-25 continue the instructions regarding elders, they contain personal counsel to Timothy. Verse 21 is especially strong. Paul lays a charge on Timothy before three witnesses: God, the Lord Jesus Christ, and the elect angels. He says: "Observe these things [the things just said and everything in the letter] without preferring one before another, doing nothing by partiality" (v. 21). Timothy is to apply all these rules without prejudice or bias. That's one charge we can translate into our time. When we treat others, either in praise of their good deeds or correction of their sins, we must do it without prejudice or bias.

The ordination of elders should not be a hasty or haphazard event. Paul cautions Timothy in verse 22 that ordaining others places him as surety for their characters. Timothy might be implicated in any sins a newly ordained elder committed. So he is warned to "keep thyself pure"—primarily by being cautious about ordaining elders.

Verses 24 and 25 relate to verse 22. They carry forward the idea of hasty ordination. Some men's sins are so evident that they must immediately be rejected as candidates. The sins of others show up later and show that the postponement of ordination was justified. The same is true of good deeds. Although this is the primary meaning of these verses, they may have reference to all Christians and their works that will be revealed at the Bema Judgment.

Many today quote 1 Timothy 5:23 as a license for "sipping." This is wrong. First, this advice is given to Timothy only. Second, drinking water was often unsafe in Eastern countries. Third, the wine of that day was unfermented grape juice (Joseph Thayer, *Greek-English Lexicon of the New Testament* [Grand Rapids: Baker Book House, 1977 edition], p. 442) that was diluted by water. Fourth, Paul prescribed a "little wine" as medicine for Timothy's "often infirmities." Timothy had a weak stomach and the polluted water was aggravating his condition. So Paul suggested a remedy.

## Servants and Masters

Possibly half the population of the Roman Empire in the first century was composed of slaves. Although slavery was contrary to the teaching of the gospel (see Galatians 3:26-28 for example), the leaders of the church did not make an issue of it. Their interest in social reform was precluded by the desire to build meaningful relationships in the church. So in 6:1 and 2 Paul speaks to yet another group: slaves.

With both slaves and masters as members of the same church, a dilemma existed: equality in the spiritual realm but superiority and inferiority in the natural realm. How are they to treat each other?

1. Slaves with non-Christian masters were to "count their own masters worthy of all honor." The words *under the yoke* reflect the attitude of non-Christian masters. They regarded slaves in the same category as cattle. But Christian slaves were to give full respect to these masters so "that the name of God and his doctrine be not blasphemed." The Christian slaves' respect for their unsaved masters would bring glory to God and would not bring reproach on His name or the gospel.

2. Slaves with Christian masters were "not to show less respect for them because they are brothers" (v. 2, *New International Version*). A Christian slave who served faithfully was expressing the love of Christ and became an even greater asset, benefiting his Christian master.

The principles taught here can be transferred to the employer/employee relationship—with restrictions. (We must remember an employee can quit if he wants, a slave could not.) But if the basic truths are applied, what a difference they will make in how we treat others.

We live in an age when relationships are shattering all around us. Nations jockey for supremacy and often consider human life expendable. Labor and management seem to constantly struggle for more benefits or greater productivity. Marriages are breaking up as communication and commitment break down. The Church must be a light in the darkness. It must lead the way in building relationships. Jesus said, "Love one another" (John 13:34).

CHAPTER 7

# Quest for True Wealth

*Read 1 Timothy 6:3-21*

DO YOU POSSESS MONEY or does money possess you? In this materialistic age the Christian must be very careful about his attitude toward and use of money. It is a perishable commodity. Those who grab for all they can get may perish with it. As we begin this study we are reminded of a true incident that happened several years ago.

Two American tourists were walking down a country road in Korea and were amused to see a boy pulling a heavy farm plow which was guided by an old man. The tourists took a picture so they could share their experience with friends back home. Later they showed the photo to a missionary who was working in the area. "Yes," he said, "it does seem to be a strange way to plow a field. I happen to know the old man well. His family is very poor. When our little church was built here in the village, the man and his family wanted to contribute to the building fund. They had no money and no grain to spare with winter coming on. So they sold their plowing ox and gave the money to the church. Until they can save enough money to buy another ox, they have to pull the plow themselves."

Though money is a major subject in the last chapter of 1 Timothy, other matters occupy Paul's final instructions.

## Folly of False Teachers

The subject matter of verses 3-5 is very similar to that found in 1:3-7. Paul identifies any man who teaches contrary to "the words of our Lord Jesus Christ, and to the doctrine which is according to godliness" as "proud, knowing nothing." Although he understands nothing, the false teacher "has an unhealthy interest in controversies and arguments" (v. 4, *New International Version*). What an indictment! Paul doesn't pull any punches. In so many words he says the false teacher is (1) conceited, (2) ignorant, (3) sick, and (4) argumentative.

Five things are listed by Paul as results of the arguments of a false teacher. They are (1) envy, (2) strife, (3) railings (or abusive speech, slander), (4) evil surmisings (suspicions), and (5) perverse disputings (constant friction or incessant wranglings). These are very picturesque words. The Holy Spirit gave them to Paul to reveal the utter folly of the false teacher.

But the descriptions are not finished. Verse 5 says that the perverse disputings or constant friction takes place among "men of corrupt minds [who are] destitute of the truth, supposing that gain is godliness." Donald Guthrie brings our attention to the last part of the verse with these words: "The concluding clause should read 'supposing that godliness is a way of gain,' or as Moffatt translates it, 'they imagine religion is a paying concern'" (*The Pastoral Epistles* [Grand Rapids: Wm. B. Eerdmans Publishing Co., 1957], p. 112). The Greek construction supports this, as does the context of the following verses.

What does all this say to us in the 20th century? As it was to Timothy, so it is to us: a warning to withdraw from false teachers who do not adhere to the wholesome words of sound doctrine. Stay away from those conceited, sick, ignorant, argumentative people who do nothing but provide abusive speech, evil suspicions, and constant friction.

## Godliness With Contentment

What a breath of fresh air verse 6 provides! "But godliness with contentment is great gain." *Godliness* is godly faith and action: the devout and practical expression of Christianity. *Contentment* is an inward sufficiency that comes from a full appropriation of God's provisions for the inner man so outward circumstances do not affect him. Paul spoke on another occasion of his own contentment. Check out Philippians 4:11.

Did Paul mean that godliness brings only spiritual blessings? Not at all. The very next verses relate this contentment with material possessions. Paul was merely repeating Jesus' teaching in the Sermon on the Mount. Christians are not to become anxious (worry or fret) about the necessities of life. A loving Heavenly Father who cares for the birds and flowers will surely take care of His children! The Christian is to seek first the kingdom of God, then all these *things* will be added. (See Matthew 6:25-34.) As Paul counsels, "Having food and raiment, let us be therewith content" (v. 8).

Godliness with contentment is great gain because "we brought [absolutely] nothing into this world [when we were born], and it is certain we can carry [absolutely] nothing out [when we die]." All the material possessions we acquire on earth must be left behind when we "shuffle off this mortal coil." Possessions are external; contentment is internal. Money is material; godliness is spiritual. Godliness and contentment will go with us when we depart. All the other "things" will be left behind.

## Money and Trouble

But those who want to get rich fall into temptation and are caught in the trap of many foolish and harmful desires, which pull them down to ruin and destruction. For the love of money is a source of all kinds of evil. Some have been so eager to have it that they have wandered away from the faith and have broken their hearts with many sorrows (vv. 9, 10, *Good News Bible*).

Piercing, instructive words!

As verse 6 began with the word *but,* so verse 9 does also. It shows a great contrast to that which immediately precedes. The opposite of godliness with contentment is greed. This greed takes one in an ever-downward spiral, not unlike a whirlpool over a deep hole. Notice the sinking direction verse 9 reveals: first a lure, then a lust, and finally total moral ruin. In the words of the Bible, first, temptation; next, hurtful lusts; finally, destruction and perdition (eternal loss).

These verses are not addressed to the already rich but to those who want to *be* rich. People who grasp and claw for this world's riches care little about others. "I want what's coming to me" is their cry—and they climb over others to satiate their greed. Their "love of money" is the root sin. It brings only trouble.

Many misquote verse 10. They think it to be, "Money is the root of all evil." If that were so, Paul's words in verses 17-19 would be a mockery. No, it is the *love* of money which is the root that produces the tree full of evil. The results of this greed are backsliding, grief, disillusionment, and heartbreaking remorse. How much better it is to put God first (godliness) and be satisfied (contentment) with the good things He provides.

## The Good Fight of Faith

Now the apostle turns again to address personal words to Timothy, his beloved son in the faith. How careful Paul is to encourage and challenge this young pastor who carries such a heavy responsibility.

> But thou, O man of God, flee these things [false teachers and greed]; and follow after righteousness, godliness, faith, love, patience, meekness. Fight the good fight of faith, lay hold on eternal life... (vv. 11, 12).

Here are Paul's famous three *F*'s: flee, follow, and fight.

The title *man of God* was given to Old Testament greats like Moses, David, and many of the prophets because of their high position and ministries. Now, Paul addresses Timothy as a "man of God" and the apostle will later refer to every believer in the same way (2 Timothy 3:17).

As men and women of God it suits our nature to run, not after riches, but after:

1. "Righteousness"—the right relationship with God which is ours through Christ.

2. "Godliness"—godly faith; the devout and practical expression of Christianity.

3. "Faith"—a trust and confidence that believes and claims God's promises.

4. "Love"—an *agape* love that is steadfast.

5. "Patience"—endurance that bears up under adversity and persecution.

6. "Meekness"—a gentleness that is the opposite of the wrangling, suspicious, envious spirit of the one who runs after riches.

"Fight the good fight of faith" reflects the figure taken from the Olympic Games where the contestant keeps on till the prize is won. In this instance the goal is "eternal life." This is not just unending life in the future but eternal life that has its source in God. It is a present possession as well as a future promise. What a worthy prize!

**The Only Potentate**

Beginning with verse 13, Paul pens one of those long sentences he is famous for. It extends to the end of verse 16, and is 92 words in the King James Version. He begins with a charge to Timothy which is found in verse 14: "Keep this commandment without spot, unrebukable [irreproachable]."

From here Paul really takes off. He seems to get carried away with his thoughts about God—who He is, and what He will do at the coming of Christ. God is the blessed and only Potentate (Sovereign), the King of kings and Lord of lords. He alone possesses immortality by His own nature, and He dwells in unapproachable light so brilliant we cannot look at it. So infinite is He, so great, so full of glory, no human being has ever seen Him. But He will display all His glory in Christ when He comes.

"Which in his times he shall show" is a striking expression. It means "at the proper time" or "in due time He will reveal." God has set a time for Christ's coming and no man knows the day or the hour. But the signs all point to the imminent return of God's Son. Let us never forget that it is His own time, not ours. He is the blessed and only Potentate; He reigns supreme and is worthy of "honor and power everlasting."

**Counsel for the Rich**

Does one have to be poor to be a Christian? No. The

rich can be Christians just as much as the poor or average man. But a rich man faces temptations the poor man doesn't. Paul instructs Timothy to command the rich to avoid arrogance and a false trust in perishable wealth. They are "to put their hope in God, who richly provides us with everything for our enjoyment" (v. 17, *New International Version*). This is true wealth.

In an age of rampant materialism the reminder of the uncertainty of riches may fall on deaf ears. But Paul isn't writing anything new. Jesus taught about the perils of materialism. (See Matthew 6:19-21, 24; 7:24-27.) Those who are wise will "put their hope in God"; those who are foolish will trust in this world's uncertain riches.

The charge or command continues in verse 18. How is a rich person to enjoy his wealth? He is to:
1. Acquire a sensitivity to the needs of others.
2. Do good works toward others.
3. Be generous and willing to share.

By doing these things the rich person will be laying a foundation for the future, and an assurance for the life to come. He does not do these things to buy his way into heaven, however. He demonstrates his love for the Lord and his fellow human beings by using his wealth in ministry to others. In the process he does not forget to share himself. Someone has said, "It is easier to give money than to give ourselves, but love requires both."

### A Final Word: "Keep"

In Paul's final admonition to Timothy in this first letter, no new note is struck. He repeats a challenge and caution that have already filled the letter. But the words selected by the Holy Spirit are significant.

"Timothy, *keep* . . . ." We saw the word *keep* earlier in

verse 14: "Keep this commandment." Now it is "keep that which is committed to thy trust." Timothy is to keep or "guard" the trust or "deposit" God has committed to his care. This primarily refers to the gospel—he is to watch over and proclaim the truth of the gospel given him by the Holy Spirit. The word *committed* appears again in two significant passages in the second letter: 2 Timothy 1:12 and 14.

Paul cautions Timothy to avoid:

1. "Profane and vain babblings"—godless, empty talk.

2. "Oppositions"—objections, contradictions, word battles.

3. "Science"—knowledge, especially that of Gnosticism.

Those who adhere to the above have "erred" and wandered away from the faith.

The challenge and caution are to us as well. We are to guard or keep those things that have been entrusted to our care. Like the runner in the marathon that starts the Olympic Games, the torch has been passed on to us. Now we must run as others have before us. We must "fight the good fight of faith" to win the prize, carrying the torch high.

The torch represents the gospel. Just as Paul passed the torch on to Timothy, so the Holy Spirit charges Christians today to carry the gospel into "all the world" (Mark 16:15). Not only pastors, missionaries, or evangelists, but all who know the Lord are to share the liberating truths of the gospel.

Are we saved? We should witness and pray for the salvation of others. Are we filled with the Spirit? Let us encourage others to claim the same fullness of the Holy Spirit. Has the Spirit revealed to our hearts the greatness of God and the glories of His coming kingdom? Then we should share these wonderful truths with others.

Jesus told a parable of a man in search of treasure in a field. When he found it he sold all his possessions to buy the land where the treasure was buried. His quest for wealth motivated him to give up everything and acquire one treasure he valued more than anything else. Christians have the greatest treasure in the world. What are we doing to help those who are searching for this treasure?

CHAPTER **8**

# Encouragement to Faithfulness

*Read 2 Timothy 1:1-18*

HAVE YOU BEEN READING THE BIBLE before reading the commentary in this book? It is very important to get God's Word in your mind and heart before considering what men have to say about it. Try an experiment. If you haven't read the first chapter of 2 Timothy, stop for a few moments to do so. As you read, pay close attention to the words. These words were inspired by the Spirit. It is Paul's most personal letter of the 13 that bear his name in the New Testament. Also, as you read, picture in your mind an old man in a Roman prison, possibly chained to a guard or to a ring in the cell wall. Think of a young man in his middle thirties to early forties reading the words you are reading. (We realize they were in another language, but the message was the same.)

With these thoughts in mind, read 2 Timothy 1:1-18. Do it now.

\* \* \* \*

What feelings seemed predominant?
What words stood out in the passage?
Was the writer more concerned about himself or his reader?
How do you think Timothy reacted to this second letter, especially since he had an earlier one that said some of the same things?

## A Second Letter

Letters are a means of communication. One of the drawbacks is that letters carry a one-way communication. The writer cannot be there to answer any questions the reader might have. The reader can misunderstand the message and respond in the wrong way. Time elapses before the error in communication is corrected. In our day this time factor may be a matter of a few days (or a few minutes if another communication device, the telephone, is used).

In A.D. 67, a letter sent from Rome to Ephesus took a long time to arrive. The time between Paul's first letter and this one was 3 or 4 years. No doubt Paul had received word about Timothy from those who visited the apostle. If there were questions about the content of the first letter, they probably were conveyed to Paul. Too, in the interim it is very possible that Paul visited Timothy in Ephesus on the way to Crete with Titus. So we can conclude that this second letter was not written to clear up misunderstandings in the first. It had a higher priority than that.

Reading the entire letter gives us a feeling that this is a spiritual "last will and testament" from Paul to his "dearly beloved son." Look at the first two verses in 1 Timothy and compare them with the first two verses in 2 Timothy. Do you notice a change in tone? What does the phrase *promise of life* in the second greeting suggest? It will help if you check out 2 Timothy 4:6, 9, 11, 13, and 21. These verses give us the occasion for this second letter. It is a personal communication from a man who was ready to pass the torch on to one who would carry it high after the apostle was gone.

## Good Memories

Paul begins this second letter with thanksgiving: "I

thank God, whom I serve from my forefathers with pure conscience" (v. 3). His mention of forefathers refers to his Jewish ancestry and heritage. Paul had served God with a pure and clear conscience for a long time. (See Acts 23:1.) Perhaps Paul mentions his forefathers because he will soon remind Timothy of his own spiritual heritage (v. 5).

The clauses that follow show a deep concern of the apostle for Timothy. They are filled with emotion:

—"Without ceasing I have remembrance of thee in my prayers night and day;
—"Greatly desiring to see thee,
—"Being mindful of thy tears,
—"That I may be filled with joy."

Evidently Timothy was an emotional young man. Paul doesn't scold him or tell him to "be a man." The apostle writes in affectionate terms about their last meeting and in expectant terms regarding their next meeting. That the apostle was praying daily for him must have encouraged Timothy greatly.

Paul writes of grandmother Lois and mother Eunice. No mention of father or grandfather! Timothy was the son of a Greek father and Jewish mother (Acts 16:1). His spiritual heritage came from the maternal side of his family tree. See 2 Timothy 3:15 for further confirmation of the influence of these godly women. Paul had no doubts about it. He said it twice in the same verse!

### Stir up the Gift

Verse 6 contains the third use of the word *remembrance*. Paul wrote: "I have remembrance of thee in my prayers" (v. 3), "I call to remembrance the unfeigned faith that is in thee" (v. 5), and "I put thee in remembrance" (v. 6). The *New International Version* says it this way: "I remind you to fan into flame the gift of God, which is in you through the laying on of my hands."

What was that "gift of God" in Timothy? You may remember that 1 Timothy 4:14 makes reference to Timothy's gift. There Paul says it was given "by prophecy, with the laying on of the hands of the presbytery." It seems this gift was a special empowering of the Holy Spirit at the time of Timothy's ordination. Paul recognized this as God's gift to Timothy so he could perform the functions required by his unique ministry. Timothy was to "stir up" or "fan into flame" this gift, which may have died because of his tendency to be intimidated by others. The next verse brings this into sharp focus.

"For God hath not given us the spirit of fear [cowardice or timidity]; but of power, and of love, and of a sound mind [self-control or self-discipline]" (v. 7). Three positives oppose one negative. The power of the Holy Spirit (see Acts 1:8), the loving spirit of Jesus, and the self-control of a God-possessed person are more than adequate to conquer timidity or cowardice.

Think of it. What God gave to Timothy is available to us today. God has not changed! His power has not abated. His love has not diminished. His willingness to give mental soundness and self-mastery as a gift to His children is not reduced in the least. God in us is greater than anything!

## Suffer for the Gospel

Although it had not happened as yet, Timothy's timidity could make him ashamed enough to stop testifying for the Lord. Remember, he was overseeing churches that were plagued by false teachers. He needed to be courageous and "fight the good fight of faith" (1 Timothy 6:12), holding high the torch of truth. Paul added that Timothy should not be ashamed of "me his prisoner" (v. 8). The aged apostle was a prisoner of the Roman government and was facing almost certain death. His suffering might be worse (at least mentally) if Timothy drew back from the close bonds of friendship that held them together.

"Join with me in suffering for the gospel, by the power of God" (v. 8, *New International Version*) is a strong challenge to young Timothy. But suffering for the right cause is commendable. Suffering for the gospel fulfills the words of Jesus. (See Matthew 5:10-12.) And the best part is that God gives the power to do it! He empowers His children to stand the test and come through with flying colors.

### The Working of Grace

The last word in verse 8, *God*, is the subject of the next 22 words. The word *grace* in verse 9 then becomes the subject for the following 22 words. Then *Jesus Christ* becomes the subject for the next 15 words. The final clause of 15 words (v. 11) has Paul ("I") as its subject. And those 110 words from verses 8 through 11 are all one sentence in the King James Version. When Paul gets started, he may change the subject, but he doesn't stop very often!

But then he has something to get excited about! Just look at some of the great words in verses 8 and 9: *God ... saved us ... called us ... according to his own purpose and grace ... given us in Christ Jesus before the world began.* And verse 10: *Jesus Christ ... abolished death*

*...brought life and immortality to light through the gospel.* That's powerful!

Paul sums up his doctrine of grace in just a few words. God's grace is embodied in His Son Jesus Christ. This grace appeared to us when Christ came into our world with a mission. (Check out John 1:14.) We gain this grace through union with Him. Our works do not earn God's grace, but it is "given us in Christ Jesus."

The grace of God in Christ took Him all the way to the cross. There, Jesus destroyed death and provided life and immortality for us by means of the gospel. The good news is that all who come to the light can have eternal life through Jesus Christ.

### God Is Able to Keep

Paul continues his testimony in verses 11 and 12. He repeats the threefold ministry God has given him: preacher, apostle and teacher. (See 1 Timothy 2:7.) Though he was a prisoner in a Roman jail, Paul never forgot his calling to the gospel ministry.

Then he writes that he is suffering because of the gospel. But this is not a sour grapes testimony. Paul doesn't languish in his abject conditions, he doesn't seek sympathy by listing all the privations he is suffering. He merely makes the statement that he is suffering because of the gospel. And he is not ashamed of that fact.

In verse 8 Paul instructed Timothy not to be ashamed to give a clear testimony for Christ. Here in verse 12 the apostle writes that he is not ashamed of the gospel. And in just a few more lines (v. 16) he will refer to a faithful disciple, Onesiphorus, who was not ashamed of Paul's chains. *Not ashamed, not ashamed, not ashamed!* Paul's repetition of a phrase certainly gives it strength. We need to respond to the call of the Spirit through this challenge today. Are we ashamed to testify for the Lord? If we are, shame on us.

Verse 12 brings Paul's testimony to a crescendo: "I know whom I have believed, and am persuaded that he is able to keep that which I have committed unto him against that day." But the question arises, what had Paul committed unto God? Was it his own soul for safe keeping? Was it his apostolic ministry now that he was about to be executed? Was it the converts he had gained? Possibly, and very probably, it was all of these and more. Paul had learned he could commit everything to God, because the Father was able to keep everything until and beyond the day of Christ's coming.

## Guard the Truth

Always conscious of Timothy's timidity, Paul instructs him as a father would a son. "Keep my words in your mind as the pattern of sound teaching, given to you in the faith and love of Christ Jesus" (v. 13, *Phillips*). This instruction involves several things.

1. Timothy is to consider Paul's words as a "pattern" for his own words. He is not to merely repeat what Paul taught, but to follow that teaching as a basis.

2. The pattern is "sound teaching." Paul had already written much about sound words and sound doctrine. These are always superior to false teaching or myths and fables.

3. Timothy is to temper the sound teaching with "faith and love." These two virtues belong together, as shown in 1 Corinthians 13:13.

4. An intimate union with Christ is necessary before faith and love are possible.

These words have great importance for us today. Although Paul wrote to Timothy in A.D. 67—a specific time and situation—the charge of verse 13 has a timeless application. We are to keep the words of the gospel as a pattern for our "sound words" which are expressed in, and tempered by, the faith and love we find in Jesus Christ. Also, the words of verse 14 are just as imperative: "Guard the good deposit that was entrusted to you—guard it with the help of the Holy Spirit who lives in us" (*New International Version*).

### Deserters—and a Friend

The final verses of chapter 1 tell us that Paul was aware of those who had turned away, and those who had stayed true. That he would write "all they which are in Asia be turned away" is incredible. Donald Guthrie suggests that Paul didn't mean *all* in a literal sense but was using hyperbole (a figure of speech expressing exaggeration).

Paul singles out Phygellus and Hermogenes for special mention. Probably these men were known to Timothy and may have been leaders in the breakaway group. Nothing else is known about them. We can only speculate that they may have been opponents of Paul's mission or authority.

But there was one who stood by Paul. Onesiphorus ("help-bringer") often "refreshed" Paul and was not ashamed of the apostle's imprisonment. This friend sought out Paul the prisoner and ministered to him on many occasions. Paul prayed that God's mercy would be poured out on this faithful "minister." (See v. 18.)

Paul wrote this second letter to encourage Timothy to be faithful. Although the apostle talked about suffering, shame, and desertion, he also spoke of joy, faith, power, love, self-control, grace, life, immortality, commitment, and the Holy Spirit. This certainly should have encouraged Timothy in his own situation. And it is more than enough to encourage us to faithfulness, no matter what our circumstances.

CHAPTER 9

# Rewards of Faithfulness

*Read 2 Timothy 2:1-13*

IT HAPPENED DURING THE 1972 SUMMER OLYMPIC GAMES in Munich. Stunned by a brutal and senseless massacre of Israeli athletes and coaches, the participants in the games regained their composure and purpose and the games went on. Though a pall seemed to shroud the usual gaiety accompanying the Olympics, the athletes competed in a serious and determined manner. Years of practice, discipline, and competition had brought them to the peak of their abilities, and each had his or her eye on the goal and the gold.

The United States premier runner in the 1972 marathon was Frank Shorter. This short, wiry, tousled-headed man had run a magnificent 25-plus miles and was ahead of the field as he approached the stadium. The TV cameras followed him through the streets and then focused on the tunnels leading into the stadium to pick him up as he entered. The TV announcers kept up an incessant stride-by-stride commentary, obviously elated by the prospect of a gold medal for the USA marathoner.

Suddenly, ... a gasp, ... then questions, ... and, finally, expressions of dismay and disgust. Another runner entered the stadium and led the way toward the tape. Spectators in the stadium thought this man clad in running gear was the leader. The TV announcers were now saying, "Who is this imposter? Where did he come from? Get that imposter off the track!"

With arms upraised this race stealer accepted the cheers of the crowds and breasted the tape several hundred yards in front of Frank Shorter. The imposter was immediately surrounded by race officials and security personnel.

TV cameras had picked up Frank Shorter as he entered the stadium. They had jockeyed between the imposter and the true leader in the race. The announcers now asked the question seemingly in the minds of every viewer: "What must Frank Shorter be thinking? Does he see the runner ahead of him? Does he know that someone tried to steal the race?"

Frank had run 26 miles, 385 yards faster than any other man on that day. Yet he wasn't sure the prized gold medal was his. At least, not at first. Only after the Olympic officials explained the attempted hoax did Frank Shorter feel the elation of winning the marathon. Even then, the victory wasn't what it should have been—all because someone didn't want to abide by the rules.

### Pass on the Good Word

> Thou, therefore, my son, be strong in the grace that is in Christ Jesus. And the things that thou hast heard of me among many witnesses, the same commit thou to faithful men, who shall be able to teach others also (2 Timothy 2:1, 2).

In the previous chapter Paul had reminded Timothy of the faith and faithfulness of his grandmother Lois and his mother Eunice. Then Paul reminded his son in the faith of his own example of faith, and urged Timothy never to be ashamed of the gospel.

In view of all this, Paul now urges Timothy not only to

be faithful, but also to be strong—strong in the grace which is in Christ. This is significant. Timothy's strength is to find its source in the grace of Christ. Newport White says: "Grace here has its simplest theological meaning, as the divine help, the unmerited gift of assistance that comes from God" (*The Pastoral Epistles, The Expositor's Greek Testament* [Grand Rapids: Wm. B. Eerdmans Publishing Co., 1952], p. 160). That same grace is available to all.

Paul's instruction in verse 2 was to encourage Timothy's faithfulness as a teacher. He was to take the words heard from Paul and commit or entrust them to faithful men. The word *faithful* carries the meaning of reliable and trustworthy. It also implies that these men were to be real believers who cherished the Christian faith and were full of faith and confidence in the Lord. Men like this would be willing to receive teaching and would become the kind of qualified, competent teachers the church needed. They would pass on the good word that Timothy would give them.

## Be a Good Soldier

The *New American Standard Bible* translates verses 3 and 4 this way:

> Suffer hardship with me, as a good soldier of Christ Jesus. No soldier in active service entangles himself in the affairs of everyday life, so that he may please the one who enlisted him as a soldier.

Paul uses three illustrations from common life to show Timothy the scope of his Christian calling. The first is that of a soldier. Often the soldier must endure the rigors and privation of battle. As a soldier of Jesus Christ, Timothy is to suffer hardship (which included persecution) as a good soldier. The term *good* means "noble, excellent." Verse 4 then goes on to point out the priority of Christian service (warfare) over "the affairs of this life."

The emphasis here is not a renunciation of family, friends, home, businesses, etc., but a caution against preoccupation with things that entangle. A similar caution can be seen in the teaching of Jesus about the seed (the Word) sown among thorns (Mark 4:18, 19). The soldier is on active duty. His first priority is obedience to his commanding officer. He does not get entangled in all sorts of projects and business enterprises that belong to civilian life. His sole purpose and intent is to bring his own desires into subjection to the will and plan of his commander.

Being a good soldier demands sacrifice, obedience, discipline, and an uncompromising loyalty. As we view the Christian life, the metaphor of soldiering lays heavy responsibility on the child of God. But if we are to please Him we must endure hardship and not become entangled in the affairs and cares of this life.

## Play by the Rules and Work Hard

The next two illustrations are of the athlete and the farmer.

> If any one competes as an athlete, he does not win the prize unless he competes according to the rules. The hardworking farmer ought to be the first to receive his share of the crops (vv. 5, 6, *New American Standard Bible*).

Paul had used all three of these metaphors in earlier letters. Especially noteworthy is 1 Corinthians 9:6, 7, 24-27 where the three are used together as here.

The athlete Paul had in mind was the one who competed in the Olympic Games. The first definite record of the Olympics dates back to 776 B.C. At that time the games were comprised of only a single race of about 200 yards. Other events were added in later years—the pentathlon (an all-around competition consisting of five events), boxing, wrestling, javelin, discus throwing, jumping contests, running races, and pancratium (a combination of boxing and wrestling).

In Paul's time the Olympic Games were well known. Athletes trained hard and long. Winners of the various contests became national heroes. If a contestant cheated to gain advantage and was discovered, he was publicly shamed and barred from the games. He was to strictly adhere to the rules.

The Christian must compete in life as the athlete strives in a contest. Self-discipline and self-control are needed. Spiritual training is vital if the Christian is to win in the struggle against sin. Laziness and a relaxing of standards will make him soft and vulnerable. But discipline, self-denial, and a goal to achieve the best make him strong and able to win. If he plays by the rules during the training period, he will compete with a chance to win. Unlike the Olympics where only one can win, every Christian who strives faithfully in the contest of life can win the crown.

The third illustration places the emphasis on hard work. The farmer works hard because he expects to partake of his crops. He must plant, cultivate, water, and wait. Then when it is time to harvest he must toil long and hard. He cannot take a vacation when the ground needs tilling or the harvest is ready. The application to the Christian and his task is obvious. Hard work and faithfulness to stay at it are essential elements in the life of one who would please God.

## Think About It!

The first part of verse 7 reminds us of that interesting word in some of the Psalms: *selah*. Some have said that *selah* is a musical annotation, an instruction to musicians at certain points in the psalm. Others have translated *selah* to be an instruction for the reader. They say it means, "Stop and think about that!"

Paul writes to Timothy: "Consider what I say; and the Lord [will] give thee understanding in all things." *Consider* means "put your mind on" and implies "grasp their meaning and apply them to your ministry." The promise of the Lord's help was probably very reassuring to Timothy. But he shouldn't expect it without effort on his part. He had to stop and think about the words Paul had written. He needed to consider the meaning and implications of the three illustrations Paul had just used. As he did this, the Lord would add understanding beyond Timothy's human ability.

A common element of promised reward is seen in these three illustrations. The soldier is sustained during the heat of battle by the thought of final victory. The athlete is encouraged to press on in the contest by the vision of the crown. The farmer is motivated to continue his hard work by the hope of the harvest. All are faithful because of a reward that will be theirs if they but persevere and reach their objectives.

The Christian struggle is not without a goal: a battle to be fought, a contest to be won, a harvest to be gathered. But each Christian should discipline himself to fight, run, or work so that at the end he will hear the words of Christ, "Well done, thou good and faithful servant."

## God's Word Isn't Bound

"Remember Jesus Christ!" Paul, possibly conscious

that Timothy may be a bit frightened by the strong words just written, now focuses on the pattern for all believers. Jesus Christ experienced suffering, persecution, and death like no other person. He is the supreme model for all those who experience suffering.

*Of the seed of David* may point to the humanity of Christ and would thus encourage Timothy to remember Jesus was a man tempted in all points like everyone else (Hebrews 4:15). *Raised from the dead* focuses attention on the victory Christ holds over sin, death, and the grave. The Resurrection is also the most prominent truth of the gospel Paul called "my gospel." Because of the Resurrection, all the other aspects of Christ's work—propitiation, redemption, justification, sanctification—are valid and effectual. Without the Resurrection His work would have been ineffectual, and our faith would be empty (1 Corinthians 15:12-19).

One other thought should have encouraged Timothy (and us). Because Jesus rose from the dead, He is alive and now intercedes for believers before the Father. Surely Paul must have been comforted with this thought when he wrote, "I am suffering even to the point of being chained like a criminal" (v. 9, *New International Version*). He connects this with his gospel witness. Paul was suffering because of his faithfulness in preaching Christ to the gentiles.

But out of the gloom of a dungeon cell, from the pen of a man chained to a Roman soldier, come the words: "But the word of God is not bound!" When the printing press was invented in Europe in the 15th century, the first pages to be printed were those of a Bible. Because printed Bibles were so costly during those times, they were chained to the pulpits to prevent theft. Very few families owned Bibles because of the immense cost. The picture of chained Bibles in the 16th century was not what Paul meant, however. What he did mean was that the preaching of the gospel was not hindered, even though he himself was in chains. Implied here is the freedom of others (like Timothy) to preach the Word of God without reservation. Even if the champion of the gospel is in chains, "the word of God is not bound."

## Salvation . . . Is in Christ

Paul writes: "I endure all things for the elect's sake, that they may also obtain the salvation which is in Christ Jesus with eternal glory" (v. 10). Who are the elect? Is it some special group? *Elect* here means "chosen" or "choice." By it Paul means all Christians. E.F. Brown says:

> The elect are those whom God has already chosen or those whom He will choose for admission into the Christian Church (*The Pastoral Epistles, Westminister Commentaries,* p. 67).

The apostle not only suffered, he also endured. He bore up under all his sufferings and trials for the sake of his fellow believers. Paul's persistence in witnessing for Christ in the face of opposition, prison, and death, would encourage them and help them to be faithful as he had been. His endurance would give them the impetus to stand their ground to the end that they might obtain the full and final salvation God had for them. (See Matthew 10:22.)

Salvation which is in Christ Jesus is both temporal and eternal. When we believe on Christ we receive salvation from sin (Acts 4:12; Ephesians 2:8, 9). But more than that we are saved *from* the penalty of sin (Romans 5:1, 9) and *to* the eternal life given us in Christ

(John 3:16; Romans 5:19-21). This is what Paul calls "eternal glory."

## God Is Faithful

Of the four "faithful sayings" (1 Timothy 1:15; 3:1; 4:9; and 2 Timothy 2:11-13), this is the longest. Many see verses 11-13 as a creedal hymn recited or sung by the Early Church. Each stanza begins with an "if we." The first two stanzas pick up the refrain "we shall," but the last two have "he" as the subject of the refrain. Let's look at each line.

"If we be dead with him"—This refers to the Christian's spiritual death to sin, his identification with Christ in His death. (See Romans 6:3-6.)

"We shall also live with him"—An identification with Christ in His death, burial, and resurrection brings a new life to the Christian. (See Romans 6:8-11.)

Some see in this reference to death and life Paul's expression of his coming martyrdom. This may be possible.

"If we suffer"—The word *suffer* here is the same word translated "endure" in verse 10. "If we endure" would be Paul's thought. Suffering is one thing, endurance is another. Endurance contains the ideas of remaining steadfast, standing our ground, and staying faithful when others are fleeing.

"We shall also reign with him"—If we endure to the end we will be given a crown and a kingdom. (See Revelation 3:21.)

"If we deny him"—Repudiate or disown him.

"He also will deny us"—Repudiate or disown us. These words reflect the teaching of Christ in Matthew 10:32, 33.

"If we believe not"—The idea of unfaithfulness underscores this phrase. It could be rendered, "If we are faithless."

"Yet he abideth faithful"—No matter if we are faithful or faithless, this does not change His character. He remains faithful forever!

"He cannot deny himself"—or as the *Good News Bible* renders it: "He cannot be false to himself." God's character will not allow Him to be anything but true to His promises. He is faithful: what He says He will do, He will do! We can put our faith in that.

## CHAPTER 10

# How to Be God's Man

*Read 2 Timothy 2:14-26*

THE BOY MISSED THE TAG AT THE PLATE. That run had just cost his team the game. Frustrated, embarrassed, and angry with himself, he threw down his catcher's mask, kicked at the plate, and stormed into the locker room. After slamming several locker doors he sat down on the bench with a towel over his head and sobbed. *I let my team down,* he told himself. *We had it in the bag and I blew it! How can I face the guys? What will the coach say?*

He was feeling his lowest when the coach came in. The boy apologized for the missed play at the plate and blubbered something about turning in his uniform and spikes. The coach didn't chew him out. Instead he came over, put his arm around the boy, and said, "C'mon, take it like a man!" But the boy wouldn't be consoled. He just sobbed all the more. It was the worst day of his life!

If it's hard for a 9-year-old boy to take defeat and embarrassment like a man, it's also difficult for grown-ups sometimes. "Be a man!" or, "Take it like a man!" is easy to say—it's another matter when you're the one in the heat of the battle.

Timothy was to some extent between a rock and a hard place. Handling the affairs of churches that were constantly threatened by false teachers and coping with his own natural timidity, Timothy needed an arm around his shoulder and an encouraging challenge, "Be a man!" But Paul did more—he told Timothy *how* to be God's man. Paul's counsel included such imperatives as: Quit quarreling about words! Study to show thyself approved! Use the truth correctly! Avoid godless chatter! Flee youthful lusts! Avoid arguments! Be gentle . . . and teach! In this chapter we want to look at some of these imperatives in depth and see their relevance for us today. In doing so we will learn how to be God's man or God's woman in our time and situation.

## Use the Truth Correctly

As we read verses 14, 15 and 16 in the King James Version, our eye is caught by the three *S*'s: *strive not, study,* and *shun.* Two are negative and one is positive. As we look at the entire passage, we find Paul gave Timothy more negatives than positives. From this we conclude that we must understand what God's man is *not* in order to comprehend what he *is.*

First, God's man must quit quarreling about words. The picture here is of time-wasting, unedifying word battles. The false teachers were experts at this. (Compare 1 Timothy 6:4.) Fighting over mere words is a waste of time: "it is of no value" (v. 14, *New International Version*), "no profit" (King James Version). Further, these word battles bring ruin (*kastastrophe*, "catastrophe") to the listeners. Timothy is to warn the "faithful men" who are teachers (v. 2) to quit quarreling about words. And we who would be true men and women of God must give up word battles that profit nothing, and that promote catastrophe in the lives of others.

Second, God's man must study to show himself "approved unto God, a workman that needeth not to be ashamed" (v. 15). Approved—ashamed, what a contrast! *Study* here is much broader than our understanding of this word as it relates to book learning. It means "be eager, be zealous, make every effort, do your utmost" to be approved by God. And if we are approved there is no reason for shame.

Third, God's man must use the truth correctly. "Rightly dividing" is literally, "straight cutting." The picture behind this phrase is the farmer who plows a straight furrow or the road builder who cuts a road across country in a straight direction. The meaning relates to what has just been said. Those who argue about words to no profit do not rightly divide the word of truth. But God's man is honest and straightforward with the Word so the Holy Spirit can use it as His tool to do God's work and as His sword to win God's battles.

When we rightly divide God's Word we use the truth correctly. Instead of twisting the Bible to fit our own ideas we handle it honestly. Instead of going to the Word for proof texts to substantiate our prejudices, we search the Bible to find out what it really teaches. We don't try to make it apply only to the other fellow. We apply it to our own lives and allow the truth to change our attitudes and actions.

### Avoid Godless Chatter

At first glance verse 16 appears to repeat verse 14. The imperative in 14 is "quit quarreling about words!" And in verse 16 it is "shun profane and vain babblings!" But verse 14 focuses on unprofitable word battles. The focus in verse 16 is godless chatter! There is a difference.

Paul warns Timothy to shun godless chatter and empty sounds. Walter Lock paraphrases it this way: "But to all these irreligious and frivolous hairsplittings give a wide berth" (*A Critical and Exegetical Commentary on the Pastoral Epistles*, p. 97). J.B. Phillips renders it this way: "Steer clear of these unchristian babblings."

Why? Because those who indulge in profane and vain babblings will become more and more ungodly. "And their word will eat as doth a canker." Not a pretty word, *canker*. It is the Greek word *gangraina* ("gangrene"), used by medical writers of Paul's day for a sore that eats into the flesh. The instruction of false teachers like Hymeneus (see 1 Timothy 1:20) and Philetus (not mentioned anywhere else in the New Testament) will eat away at the hearer like gangrene eats at an infected body. The only prevention is to avoid men like this at all costs.

Paul points out that Hymeneus and Philetus have "wandered away from the truth. They say that the resurrection has already taken place, and they destroy the faith of some" (v. 18, *New International Version*). They were probably explaining the Resurrection in a spiritual sense, equating it with the life of Christ coming into a person at the new birth. This insidious teaching destroyed the true meaning of the Resurrection for some in the Ephesian churches. Earlier Paul wrote a lengthy discourse to answer this false teaching in the church at Corinth (1 Corinthians 15).

## God Knows Those Who Are His

> Nevertheless the foundation of God standeth sure, having this seal, The Lord knoweth them that are his. And, Let every one that nameth the name of Christ depart from iniquity (v. 19).

The word *nevertheless* is a transitional term. After the negative tone and content of verses 16-18, the apostle strikes a positive and encouraging note.

*Foundation* could refer to several things: Christ, the apostles, the Church, the truth. Because of its clear use in Ephesians 2:20, the *Church* seems the best choice. The presence of God's "seal" makes the difference between the false and true Christian.

Two quotations from the Old Testament make up this seal; the first reflects ownership, the second responsibility. "The Lord knoweth them that are his" is a paraphrase of Numbers 16:5. That text comes from the narrative of Korah's rebellion. Moses made it clear that God would show who was His and who was not. "Let every one that nameth the name of Christ depart from iniquity" is a reflection of Moses' words in Numbers 16:26—again from the Korah narrative.

Both of these concepts were taught by Jesus. (See Matthew 7:22; Luke 13:27.) They give us two principles regarding the Church. First, the Church consists of those who belong to God. Second, the Church consists of those who have departed from unrighteousness. This doesn't mean they are perfect. It means they have turned their backs on sin and are walking toward the glorious perfection found in the Son of God. It may be a struggle sometimes, but God knows who is sincerely seeking to find and do His perfect will.

### Illustration: Useful Vessels

In verses 20 and 21 Paul introduces an illustration to show the different functions of people in the Church. The "great house" is the Church and the vessels of gold and silver ("some to honor") and the vessels of wood and earth ("some to dishonor") are the different types of people in the Church. Some are prepared for leadership roles, others are fitted to more menial tasks. Both have their place and function in the Church.

"If a man therefore purge himself from these" (probably the false teachings mentioned earlier), "he shall be a vessel unto honor" (v. 21). This is described in three ways. First, he is "sanctified" (set apart for a holy purpose). Second, he is "meet for the master's use" (available and useful for God's work). And third, he is "prepared unto every good work" (ready to do any and every good work). This is the kind of vessel God is looking for. He wants useful vessels, not just beautiful vessels.

## Flee Youthful Lusts

Beginning at verse 22, Paul returns to the imperatives that show Timothy how to be God's man. Consider how J.B. Phillips paraphrases the one so familiar in the King James Version:

> Turn your back on the turbulent desires of youth and give your positive attention to goodness, integrity, love and peace in company with all those who approach the Lord in sincerity.

Here we find one negative and four positives. Timothy is to flee youthful lusts and pursue *righteousness* (Phillips' "goodness" is an inadequate translation), *integrity* (including faithfulness, obedience), *love* (see 2 Timothy 1:7, 13), and *peace*. (Check out Matthew 5:9.) It is not enough to run away from wrong; the Christian must run after what is good.

This instruction repeats 1 Timothy 6:11. So Paul isn't telling Timothy anything new. In the 3 to 4 years between letters, the need for this imperative had not diminished. And in the 1900-plus years since the Holy Spirit first inspired Paul to write these words, the need for this instruction is still apparent.

The "turbulent desires of youth" are not relegated *only* to the youth. (Remember, Timothy was in his late thirties or early forties.) The Christian must constantly keep his passions in check. A permissive society is no excuse for relaxing the standard of holiness God expects from His people. The everybody-is-doing-it syndrome is not a license for exercising "freedom." The Word tells every Christian: "Flee ... youthful lusts!"

Galatians 6:10 says: "As we have therefore opportunity, let us do good unto all men, especially unto them who are of the household of faith." The Christian is to do good to all; he is to follow righteousness, faith, love, and peace. If these virtues are his motivation as well as his goals, he will be properly related to God and his neighbor.

All these virtues are to be sought in the company of those "that call on the Lord out of a pure heart" (v. 22). The Christian will find his strength and joy among those in the church fellowship. There is very little of that kind of support in society. But neither is he to neglect his witness of righteousness, integrity, love, and peace among those outside the household of faith.

## Avoid Arguments

Paul cautions Timothy: "Don't have anything to do with foolish and stupid arguments, because you know they produce quarrels" (v. 23, *New International Version*). Again, this is not a new instruction (see 1 Timothy 1:4; 4:7; 6:20; 2 Timothy 2:16). But to be God's man, Timothy must make a conscious effort to sidestep the divisive, unprofitable, foolish, and ignorant questions that surely would come (and no doubt had already come). He must refuse to discuss them because all they ever do is produce quarrels. God's man is not to be argumentative or quarrelsome. That is contrary to the virtues listed in the previous verses and the requirements given in the following verses.

So often it is easy for the person who knows he is right to say, "Yes, but ...!" and then tell the other person how it really is. But that's not what Christ did. And that's not what He wants from those today who would be God's man or woman. He wants something special from each of them.

**Be Gentle . . . and Teach**

The final verses of this chapter give us a clear and unmistakable picture of how to be God's man. Pause and read 2 Timothy 2:24-26. God's man:

1. "Must not strive"—He doesn't get embroiled in quarrels or word battles.

2. Must "be gentle"—Gentle and kind even when he has to point out a fault. "Unto all men"—He must treat each person the same and avoid favoritism.

3. Must be "apt to teach"—Skillful in teaching; "a skilled and suitable teacher" (*The Amplified Bible*).

4. Must be "patient"—Able to bear resentment against his person, putting up with evil in a forbearing spirit.

5. Must in "meekness" instruct "those that oppose themselves"—The meaning here is a gentleness that shows kindness, self-control, and a humility that is willing to forgive. Those who oppose themselves are people who set themselves up as opponents to God's servant by their false teachings or wrong standards.

Timothy is to demonstrate all these qualities as God's man. But there is something more. When he takes the positive, gentle, patient approach to his teaching, he will find that God may bring men to repentance and a knowledge of the truth (v. 25). This is what it's all about: unregenerate men and women coming to the knowledge of the truth of God's liberating Word.

But even more tremendous results can be seen. If Timothy will take this approach, and if his hearers will repent, "they will come to their senses and escape from the trap of the devil, who has taken them captive to do his will" (v. 26, *New International Version*). So not only does Timothy benefit personally from striving to be God's man, but also those who hear and respond receive deliverance and blessing.

CHAPTER **11**

# Trends of the Times

*Read 2 Timothy 3:1-13*

"IT WAS THE BEST OF TIMES; it was the worst of times." That line begins Charles Dickens' classic, *A Tale of Two Cities.* It also describes the transition we see from what Paul has just written to what he now writes.

Paul has just encouraged Timothy to be gentle and teach men the truth. If he does, God will show His mercy by giving these men repentance and recovery from Satan's captivity—the "best of times." The gospel was not hindered. Though Paul was in a Roman prison, men like Timothy and others were proclaiming the gospel and sinners were being saved.

But chapter 3 is a different story. Paul writes to Timothy about the "worst of times." The language is vital—and frightening. The picture Paul paints is not pleasant at all. The first 13 verses reveal a scene we would rather not see. Paul writes of the evil characters and activities of people in the last days. He calls these days "perilous times" and lists almost a score of evil attitudes and actions. Amid all this Paul holds out one bright spot—and illustrates it from his own life and ministry.

So... "it was the best of times; it was the worst of times." By studying this portion of God's Word in 2 Timothy 3:1-13, we will gain a better understanding of what the Holy Spirit reveals through Paul regarding the trends of the times.

## Perilous Times

Paul warns Timothy: "This know also, that in the last days perilous times shall come" (v. 1). What are the "last days" Paul is writing about? We see that this term is used in Joel 2:28 and is quoted by Peter on the Day of Pentecost (Acts 2:17). In these instances, *last days* refers to the entire Messianic Age—all the days between the first and second comings of Christ. But here it has a narrower meaning. *Last days* in this context refers to the last days of this age, before the Second Coming. (Compare 2 Peter 3:3 and Jude 18.)

We must remember that the Early Church considered the Second Coming imminent. And, although it is now almost two millennia later, Christ's coming is still imminent. We must view our day as part of the "last days" Paul writes about.

He warns that perilous times will come. The meaning of *perilous* is "hard, difficult, terrible, hard to bear, troublesome, dangerous." They are times of stress; times hard to live in and bear up under. Perhaps it is difficult for those who live in an affluent society to grasp the concept of perilous times. But our inability to understand does not lessen the reality that these perilous times are coming. The next passage gives us insight into the godlessness that will mark these last days.

## All Kinds of Evil

As we read verses 2-4 we are struck—if not shocked—by the gross evil prevalent in the last days. Paul writes that "men shall be":

1. *Lovers of their own selves.* The basic idea in this

phrase is "selfishness, self-centeredness." It, along with the next, gives the key to the entire list. Whenever people allow self-love to rule their hearts instead of love for God and others (see Mark 12:29-31), all kinds of evil follow.

2. *Covetous*. Many translations render it "lovers of money." This parallels the first phrase and reveals the two keys to the rest of the list of 18 evils. *The Amplified Bible* gives a vivid word picture: "Lovers of money and aroused by an inordinate (greedy) desire for wealth."

3. *Boasters*. "Braggarts."

4. *Proud*. "Arrogant, haughty," literally "showing oneself above others." These two go together. J. H. Bernard translates these two words as "*boastful, haughty*, the former term referring especially to *words*, the latter to thoughts" (*The Pastoral Epistles*, p. 130).

5. *Blasphemers*. This describes those who are "evil-speaking, slanderous, and abusive" people. Their blasphemous words are directed to God and their fellowmen. They show disregard for the feelings of others and hurl insults because it's their nature to be abusive. An antidote for this is given in Proverbs 15:1.

6. *Disobedient to parents*. The ancient world put great emphasis on respect for, and obedience to, parents. One of the Ten Commandments spells it out in no uncertain terms. Viewing the contemporary scene, one wonders if there ever was a day when disobedience and abuse of parents were more prevalent than today.

7. *Unthankful*. Men will (and do) refuse to recognize the debt they owe to God and their fellowmen. Ingratitude is a sin that hurts because it is so easy to express thankfulness.

8. *Unholy*. This word describes the person who has no fellowship with God. He is living a secular life by

following the dictates and passions of an unrestrained, pleasure-seeking life-style.

9. *Without natural affection.* "Without family affection." It is natural for a child to love his parents and parents to love their children. But in the last days men will be so self-centered that even the closest ties will mean nothing to them.

10. *Trucebreakers.* The idea here is that men will be "irreconcilable, implacable." They will refuse to make any truce with those who oppose them. They will refuse to forgive wrongs done to them. They will not work with people who do not agree with them in every detail. What a sad state of affairs. But just look around and think of how many personal, national, and international situations reflect this godless characteristic.

11. *False accusers.* "Slanderers." It is one thing to steal a man's possessions; it is quite another and much worse to steal his reputation by the sin of slander. People who wouldn't dream of stealing, think little of passing on some story that ruins another's good name. Someone has said there is enough slander in churches to make the recording angel weep as he records it in heaven.

12. *Incontinent.* "Without self-control, lacking self-discipline." This term describes the weak man who is easily led into sin. The habitual sinner got that way because he did not control some habit or desire. It mastered him and he became its slave.

13. *Fierce.* "Not tame, brutal, savage." This characteristic normally applies to animals. But Paul uses it to show that men in the last days will be animalistic in nature. They will become savage and lose the sensitivity and sympathy that humans should exhibit toward one another.

14. *Despisers of those that are good.* "Haters of good (both good things and good persons)." Fellowship with goodness is shunned by men with warped motives and pursuits. Jesus said, "Men loved darkness rather than light, because their deeds were evil" (John 3:19).

15. *Traitors.* "Treacherous."

16. *Heady.* "Rash, hasty, reckless."

17. *High-minded.* "Conceited." These three are linked by a common meaning. *The Amplified Bible* reads: "[They will be] treacherous (betrayers), rash [and] inflated with self-conceit." The common thread in these three is the devious, rash, impulsive thoughts and actions of last-day men toward others.

18. *Lovers of pleasure more than lovers of God.* This final characteristic links us again to the first one. Because men are "lovers of their own selves" they have enthroned self and pushed God out of their lives. Therefore, they have become "lovers of sensual pleasures and vain amusements more than, and rather than, lovers of God" (v. 4, *The Amplified Bible*).

## Showing a Form of Godliness

Yet Paul writes that these men in the "last days" are religious—"having a form of godliness, but denying the power thereof" (v. 5). They go through all the correct motions and maintain all the external forms, but they know nothing of true Christianity as a dynamic power to change lives.

That men will hold to religion in the last days is understandable. Think of all the benefits religion brings: fellowship, respectability, a common cause, and a certain amount of guilt-release from the burden of sin. Many well-meaning people put stock in a works religion: do good to others, pay your debts, attend church, honor

God, and obey civil law. In doing these things they think God is pleased.

God wants to change men's lives by the power of the gospel. He wants men to accept forgiveness and cleansing for sin, and to receive the righteousness of Christ by faith. God desires much more than just a form of godliness; He wants the reality of righteousness.

## Silly and Sensual Women

After the long list of the characteristics of last-day men, Paul instructs Timothy:

> From such turn away. For of this sort [from the ranks of just such men] are they [false teachers] which creep into houses, and lead captive silly women laden with sins, led away with divers lusts, ever learning, and never able to come to the knowledge of the truth (vv. 5-7).

Paul was not a first-century male chauvinist. As stated earlier, women in Paul's day did not have the opportunity to become educated. The false teachers often went from house to house teaching "new and deep truths." In this way they gained control over the women and made them feel important.

The description of these women is sad. They were silly, sinful, and sensual. *Silly* means literally "little," but probably denotes feebleness or moral and intellectual weakness. *Laden with sins* suggests an acute state of guilt consciousness. *Led away with divers lusts* suggests that these women were easily "swayed and led away by various evil desires and seductive impulses" (v. 6, *The Amplified Bible*). They were always ready to listen to anyone who would teach them "deep truths." Then they could pose as enlightened, learned females. But verse 7 says they remained ignorant of the truth.

Intellectual curiosity without spiritual earnestness is dangerous. Wanting to hear something of a sensational nature should not interest the Christian who knows the Truth. Paul warned his Ephesian readers about following every wind of doctrine (Ephesians 4:14), and Christians today must hold to the Truth and say, "It is enough!"

## Opposers of the Truth

Jannes and Jambres are not mentioned in the Old Testament. But Jewish tradition says they are two of the Egyptian magicians who withstood Moses and Aaron when they came to Pharaoh (Exodus 7:10-13). Paul says that false teachers are like these magicians.

1. *They resist the truth.* Just as Jannes and Jambres opposed Moses, so these men oppose the truth of God—in Paul's day—and in ours.

2. *They are men of corrupt minds.* The meaning here is "depraved, utterly corrupted." Such a mind cannot produce a clean, God-honoring thought.

3. *They are reprobate concerning the faith.* Reprobate means "not standing the test, worthless, base, rejected." They cannot be trusted to teach the truth.

Verse 9 should have encouraged Timothy. Paul writes: "But they will not get very far because, as in the case of those men, their folly will be clear to everyone" (*New International Version*). Here Paul uses the Old Testament contrast of truth and folly (seen especially in Proverbs). Because these teachers have opposed the truth and rejected the faith, their end is utter folly which will be evident to everyone. Truth will triumph in the end.

## Persecution of the Godly

A new paragraph begins at verse 10. As Paul has done

so frequently in his letters to Timothy, he again draws on his own experience to encourage and instruct his son in the faith. Stop here and reread 2 Timothy 3:10-13.

How many things does Paul list in verses 10 and 11? How many places does he list? It's nine and three respectively. This shows the Jewish mind-set toward trilogies. It also means that Paul's list is not exhaustive but merely representative.

1. *Doctrine.* First in the list and first in priority, Paul has constantly written about doctrine. (See 1 Timothy 1:3, 10; 4:6, 13, 16; 5:17; 6:1, 3.) But doctrine must be linked with life. So the next six in the list bring out the practical impact of Paul's life and witness upon Timothy.

2. *Manner of life.* Paul's life-style was well known to Timothy since Timothy traveled with Paul extensively.

3. *Purpose.* "Chief aim" or "goal." This is reflected in Philippians 3:8-11.

4. *Faith.* Can also mean faithfulness and may include Paul's loyalty to the Christian faith.

5. *Long-suffering.* "Patience," a quality Paul had to show repeatedly toward his opponents—and his converts.

6. *Charity.* A holy, self-giving love that comes from God himself. Human love is not sufficient; we need *agape*.

7. *Patience.* "Steadfast endurance."

8. *Persecutions.*

9. *Afflictions.* These last two speak of the reactions Paul received because of his missionary work in Antioch, Iconium, and Lystra (Acts 13 and 14).

"But out of them all the Lord delivered me!" This is the high point of the entire chapter. Paul exclaims that God is his rescuer, his deliverer. Out of this wonderful word of faith and confidence, Paul then declares: "Yea, and all that will live godly in Christ Jesus shall suffer persecution" (v. 12).

One final trend of the times is found in verse 13: evil men will become extremely evil. Deception will be a vicious cycle and deceivers will deceive while being themselves deceived. There is no promising future for the man who refuses to accept God's way. But for the Christian, even though persecution may come, there is deliverance just as God has promised.

CHAPTER **12**

# The Value of Scripture

*Read 2 Timothy 3:14 to 4:5*

D.L. MOODY ONCE SAID: "What we need today is men who believe in the Bible from the crown of their heads to the soles of their feet: who believe in the whole of it, the things they understand, and the things they do not understand."

Controversy over the Bible's inerrancy has raged for several years. Late in 1978 this issue brought together 284 people, mostly theologians, to define inerrancy. The result of the 3-day meeting was a 4,825-word document called "The Chicago Statement on Biblical Inerrancy." The core of the document is a "Short Statement" of five governing principles. They are:

1. God, who is Himself Truth and speaks truth only, has inspired Holy Scripture in order thereby to reveal Himself to lost mankind through Jesus Christ as Creator and Lord, Redeemer and Judge. Holy Scripture is God's witness to Himself.

2. Holy Scripture, being God's own Word, written by men prepared and superintended by His Spirit, is of infallible divine authority in all matters upon which it touches: it is to be believed, as God's instruction, in all that it affirms; obeyed, as God's command, in all that it requires; embraced, as God's pledge, in all it promises.

3. The Holy Spirit, its divine Author, both authenticates it to us by His inward witness and opens our minds to understand its meaning.

4. Being wholly and verbally God-given, Scripture is without error or fault in all its teaching, no less in what it states about God's acts in creation and the events of world history, and about its own literary origins under God, than in its witness to God's saving grace in individual lives.

5. The authority of Scripture is inescapably impaired if this total divine inerrancy is in any way limited or disregarded, or made relative to a view of truth contrary to the Bible's own; and such lapses bring serious loss to both the individual and the Church.

As we study this portion of Paul's letter to Timothy, we will focus on the golden text of inerrancy: 2 Timothy 3:16. But let's examine the context first.

### Able to Make You Wise

One very important value attributed to the Bible is its ability "to make thee wise unto salvation through faith which is in Christ Jesus" (3:15). The words:"knowing of whom thou hast learned them; and that from a child thou hast known the holy Scriptures," refer back to 1:5 where Timothy's grandmother Lois and his mother Eunice are identified as his "teachers." They taught him the Old Testament discipline of obedience to God, and pointed him to the coming Messiah. As he responded in faith, Timothy received the salvation God had promised in the Old Testament and provided in the person of His Son Jesus Christ.

Timothy is told to "continue in what you have learned and have become convinced of" (v. 14, *New International Version*). The word *continue* includes the meaning of "abide, stay." Paul made this point earlier (1 Timothy 4:16). The idea of perseverance in the faith comes through very strongly in these letters to Timothy. The Christian cannot slide along nonchalantly or be inconsistent. Continuance in the things one has learned and accepted is vitally important to spiritual well-being. The charge to Timothy is a challenge to every Christian. Perseverance is imperative.

### All Scripture Is "God-breathed"

The phrase *given by inspiration of God* is one word in the Greek, *theopneustos,* which means "God-breathed." Inspiration is the process God used to produce "all Scripture." This means that by the divine inbreathing of the Holy Spirit, men spoke or wrote the actual words of God. This applies to original documents called autographs: these bear the special marks of divine inspiration.

But some will ask: "Where are the original documents now?" Archaeological discoveries have not produced one single autograph. For some reason God has not seen fit to preserve the originals, possibly to prevent men from worshiping them. But does that mean we cannot trust the Bible versions we do have? Not at all. While there are minor differences among the manuscript copies, they are in perfect agreement concerning the major doctrines of the Christian faith. Though there are variations among the copies, not one major doctrine of Christianity depends on a disputed verse. And that includes 2 Timothy 3:16!

"All Scripture is given by inspiration of God" does not tell us how the divine inspiration took place, however. It is Peter who declares: "No prophecy of the Scripture is of any private interpretation" (2 Peter 1:20). This means no part of the Bible came as any man's individual or personal interpretation or explanation.

> For the prophecy [the speaking for God] came not in old time by the will [desire or wish] of man: but holy men of God spake as they were moved [moved along, borne along] by the Holy Ghost (2 Peter 1:21).

The Bible—both Old and New Testaments—can be trusted. It is the Word of God, recorded by men who were inbreathed by the Holy Spirit as they wrote.

## The Profits of Scripture

The second half of verse 16 lists four profitable uses of Scripture.

1. *Doctrine* (or "teaching"). Timothy had learned the precepts that made him wise unto (helped him understand) salvation. The value of Scripture for teaching is that it is the truth, the whole truth, and nothing but the truth. It can be totally trusted as sound doctrine.

2. *Reproof* (or "conviction of sin"). Men can be rebuked and convicted of sin by both hearing and reading the Bible. A sense of guilt can prompt the sinner to reach out for God's mercy. When he realizes his need, the Holy Spirit can lead him to other passages that show him the way of salvation.

3. *Correction* (including "restoration" and "improvement"). *The Amplified Bible* translates this phrase, "for correction of error and discipline in obedience." Literally, *correction* means "restoration to an upright position or a right state." The value of Scripture here is that it brings man back into a proper relationship with God.

4. *Instruction* ("training, discipline") *in righteousness.* This word originally referred to the training used in the rearing of a child. Here the training is "in righteousness [that is, in holy living, in conformity to God's will in thought, purpose and action]" (v. 16, *The Amplified Bible*). The profit here is found in the fact that the Bible gives God's view of righteousness. This supersedes man's conception of what God wants from His creation.

As *all* Scripture is God-breathed, so *all* Scripture is profitable. It is up to each individual to accept the Bible as his or her rule of faith and conduct. If a person does not take it as his standard, what standard does he have? Changing human customs? changing pronouncements of theologians, popes, or philosophers? changing theories of science? or man's changing feelings and ideas? All these are woefully inadequate. Only the unchanging, trustworthy, God-inspired Word is a true guide for faith and conduct.

### The Purpose of Scripture

All these uses of Scripture have a purpose: "that the man of God may be perfect, thoroughly furnished unto all good works" (v. 17). The word *perfect* means "fit, capable," and the phrase *thoroughly furnished unto all good works* means "fully equipped for every kind of good work." (Compare 2 Timothy 2:21.)

The primary application of verse 17 is to Timothy. *Man of God* is uniquely applicable to a minister and we must remember that this letter was written to Timothy. The context relates to Timothy (especially vv. 14, 15 and 4:1 where *thou* and *thee* are addressed to him). But after understanding the primary application to Timothy, it is not wrong to ask, "Is there a timeless principle here for everyone?"

As verse 16 relates the profits of Scripture and connects these to the purpose of Scripture (v. 17), a general application can be made. Any person who wishes to become fit and equipped for every good work should search the Scriptures. They will reprove, correct, and instruct him in righteousness.

### What to Do With the Word

Now we come to Paul's final challenge to Timothy.

The first five verses of 2 Timothy 4 are a key passage of this entire letter. Because Paul was convinced of the imminent return of Christ (v. 1; compare 1 Thessalonians 4:16, 17), he told Timothy to "preach the word; be instant in season, out of season; reprove, rebuke, exhort with all long-suffering and doctrine" (v. 2). These exhortations are applicable to all ministers.

1. *Preach the Word.* The preacher is not to voice his own opinions but to proclaim God's eternal Word. Only God's truth has the answer to the needs and hurts of mankind.

2. *Be instant in season, out of season.* The minister must always be ready to serve, whether he feels like it or not. The call to serve others is not for seasonal workers or temporary help.

3. *Reprove.* The spiritual leader must correct when the situation warrants it. He should use the Word to "convict" the offender.

4. *Rebuke.* Similar to reprove, it means "censure, admonish." These two are the negatives, showing the need for correction and discipline among God's people.

5. *Exhort.* The minister is to encourage and comfort others by his words. This is one of his greatest opportunities as a servant of Christ and of God's people.

All of this is to be done "with great patience and careful instruction" (v. 2, *New International Version*). Here are both the manner ("patience") and the method ("careful instruction") the preacher must use as he applies the Word to everyday situations and church problems. If he misuses the Word or acts without love, his service is ineffective.

### Truth and Itching Ears

In the next two verses (3 and 4) Paul warns Timothy

of a time when men will not put up with, bear with, or listen to "sound doctrine." Instead, because they have "itching ears," they will gather a bunch of false teachers around them to tell them fables, myths, and fictional stories. These people are not interested in the Word or the truth; they want to satisfy their own lusts or desires.

The idea behind the term *itching ears* is that of entertainment. These people want to have their ears tickled with sensational, stimulating, or satisfying oratory. So opportunistic teachers take advantage of these carnal people and give them what they want: intellectual entertainment. This problem of Timothy's day is still with us. There are a lot of people today who have "itching ears."

Because some will not put up with sound doctrine (a key phrase in Paul's letters to Timothy), they will "turn away their ears from the truth, and shall be turned unto fables" (v. 4). The rejection of truth is a serious matter. Once this is done, what is left? Anything less than the truth is totally inadequate. And Paul shows the folly of this by calling them fables (compare 1 Timothy 1:4; 4:7). The carnal heart prefers man-made fables to God's truth. What a tragedy!

### Four Words of Urgency

"But watch thou in all things, endure afflictions, do the work of an evangelist, make full proof of thy ministry" is perhaps the key verse of this entire second letter. Paul was so conscious of the brevity of his own life that this "last will and testament," to Timothy closes with four words of extreme urgency. Let's look at each of them for meaning and present application.

1. *Watch . . . in all things.* The meaning here is that of self-control and self-possession. It might be paraphrased

like this: "Be self-possessed and keep well balanced under all circumstances." Timothy was to "keep his head" in the heat of the battle against sin and false doctrine among the Ephesian churches. By his example (see 1 Timothy 4:12) he was to lead others to a place of self-possession and a balanced Christian life. This word is just as applicable today. The people of God must be self-possessed and well balanced in all circumstances.

2. *Endure afflictions.* Timothy has already been urged to "endure hardness, as a good soldier of Jesus Christ" (2:3). Paul has just referred to his own afflictions (3:11). The meaning here is "accept whatever suffering comes." Being a Christian costs something and the one who would serve Christ should pay the price without grumbling or regret.

3. *Do the work of an evangelist.* The word *evangelist* occurs only two other times: Acts 21:8 and Ephesians 4:11. Both refer to the office of an evangelist. The duties of this office are suggested by the meaning of the term: "announce the good news, preach the gospel." Though he had important administrative responsibilities, Timothy was not to neglect a bold declaration of the gospel. So, too, today's Christian must be a bold witness, sharing the good news with others.

4. *Make full proof of thy ministry.* The core idea here is fulfillment. *The Amplified Bible* renders it: "Fully perform all the duties of your ministry." Timothy is to pack his ministry full with the things Paul has been exhorting him to do in these two letters. The Christian today may not be in a pastoral ministry like Timothy was, but every believer is a "minister"—to the Lord and to others. Each Christian should fill his life to the full and "leave nothing undone that [he or she] ought to do."

CHAPTER **13**

## Foes, Friends, and Final Words

*Read 2 Timothy 4:6-22*

THE RELATIVES GATHERED in the lawyer's office. You could tell a great deal by looking at their eyes. Some had beady eyes that showed a distrust for anyone and everyone. Some had shifty eyes that gave a hint of greed. A few had tearful eyes that revealed both sorrow and guilt at the same time. No one spoke to each other, but their thoughts were focused on that one thing which meant so much to all of them—Uncle Martin's will.

The lawyer began the reading of Uncle Martin's last will and testament: "I, Martin Levy, being of sound and disposing mind and memory and above the age of twenty-one years, do hereby revoke all other prior Wills and Codicils by me at any time heretofore made...." As the lawyer droned on through the preliminary statements the beady eyes and the shifty eyes kept moving around the room, focusing first on one relative, then another. The tearful eyes were dabbed by handkerchiefs held low enough so as to peek out at the others.

The tension in the room became almost unbearable. The relatives hadn't gathered to mourn or honor the dead but to squabble over the estate. It wasn't a pretty sight. It appeared as if the fight was just about to begin.

What a contrast we find in the last will and testament of the apostle Paul. He writes to Timothy concerning eternal rewards.

## A Crown of Righteousness

> For I am now ready to be offered, and the time of my departure is at hand. I have fought a good fight, I have finished my course, I have kept the faith: henceforth there is laid up for me a crown of righteousness, which the Lord, the righteous judge, shall give me at that day: and not to me only, but unto all them also that love his appearing (vv. 6-8).

The imagery these words conveyed to Timothy is hidden from the modern western mind. In verse 6 Paul uses two figures that are full of meaning. They both show the glorious, triumphant, and unique view of death that is the Christian's.

*For I am now ready to be offered* may be rendered: "As for myself, I already am being outpoured (as a drink offering)." The drink offering of the Old Testament was a second cup of wine poured out after the other offerings were made. Two possible meanings should be considered. (1) Christ made the one sacrifice that fulfilled the Old Testament types of sacrifices and offerings. Paul, who came later "as one born out of due time" (1 Corinthians 15:8), viewed his life as a secondary sacrifice, poured out in accompaniment with Christ's. (2) Paul had given everything in sacrifice to the Lord: his time, his talents, his strength, his mind, his heart, and his will. The only thing left was his life. Now he was even ready to do that.

*The time of my departure is at hand* gives a beautiful picture of Christian death. The word *departure* in this clause literally means "loosing" (as a ship from its moorings or an animal from its tether) or "dismantling" (as of a tent). Both pictures have deep significance. The loosing connotes freedom. Death brings us into a new existence that frees us from the restrictions of our present life. The striking metaphor of a tent reminds us that the body is but a physical tabernacle for the real life inside. Peter used the same imagery when he referred to his own departure (2 Peter 1:14, 15).

Three more pictures are described in verse 7. They each relate to the Olympic Games, a figure Paul used repeatedly.

1. *I have fought a good fight.* "I have contended (as for a prize) in the good contest" would be an expanded literal translation. (Check out Philippians 3:14).

2. *I have finished my course* (or "race"). Notice Paul does not say, "I have won my race." Having begun, all he wanted was to finish. A famous man was asked if his biography could be written before he died. He absolutely forbade it saying, "I have seen so many men fall out on the last lap."

3. *I have kept the faith.* Two meanings are possible here. The first is from the games. "I have kept the rules" suggests Paul had not "fouled out" and been disqualified from the race. The second is from the business world. "I have kept the conditions of the contract" suggests that Paul had never once violated the terms of his apostleship. He had never let his Lord down.

All three of these figures have relevance for Christians today. The statements themselves give us a goal to shoot for—and the prize is a crown of righteousness. The "crown" here is not a royal crown, but the laurel wreath given to the winner of the race. The word *henceforth* means "already." Paul knew the crown was already his. Then he adds that the Lord, the righteous Judge (of the contest), is waiting to award a crown to everyone who loves and longs for His appearing (Christ's second coming).

## A Spiritual Dropout

As Paul begins his list of co-workers, a blight appears. Much has been said and written about Demas, and verse 10 of 2 Timothy 4 is a sad epitaph: "Demas hath forsaken me, having loved this present world." Paul has mentioned Demas twice before (Colossians 4:14 and Philemon 24). Speculate for a moment on the reasons Demas became a dropout.

1. He may have begun following Christ without counting the cost. Perhaps in his youthful zeal to take up a cause, Demas' commitment was not as deep as it should have been. Emotion may have swept him into a shallow commitment that resulted in his discipleship being weak.

2. He may have become affected by years of unpopularity, sacrifice, persecution, and loneliness. When imprisonment came, it could have been the last straw in a life-style that ran an opposite course to what Demas had expected. Having begun the race with enthusiasm, Demas may have dropped out because of mental and physical exhaustion.

3. Putting speculation aside, the primary reason is given in Holy Scripture: he "loved this present world [age, life]." Demas failed to see the long view. Creature comforts of this life took precedence over communion with Christ. The ways of the world held more appeal for Demas than the way of the Cross.

Paul uses the word *love* to show great contrast. All those who love Christ's appearing will receive a crown of righteousness. But Demas loved this present life and deserted Paul, thus becoming a spiritual dropout. There's a profound lesson in this for all of us.

Two others are mentioned in verse 10: Crescens and Titus. These men did not desert Paul; they were sent to

Galatia and Dalmatia respectively. Nothing else is mentioned of Crescens in Scripture. Titus, having completed his ministry in Crete (see Titus 1:5), has been dispatched to his new assignment on the eastern shore of the Adriatic Sea, north of Macedonia.

## People and Property

Paul, writing to his "son in the faith," includes personal matters in this last letter to Timothy. The apostle refers to special friends.

1. *Only Luke is with me.* The faithful, beloved physician and longtime traveling companion is the one person who has stayed with him. Very possibly it was Luke who acted as Paul's secretary in the actual writing of this final letter. Also, as a doctor, Luke could minister to Paul who was both aging and ailing because of the earlier beatings, stonings, and deprivations he had suffered.

2. *Take Mark, and bring him with thee.* Having flunked out earlier (Acts 13:13; *John* refers to John Mark), we now see Paul valuing the later efforts of Mark. He commends him by saying, "He is profitable to me for the ministry." Perhaps Paul wanted to counsel Mark and give him an assignment like that of Crescens, Titus, and Tychicus (vv. 10, 12). In any event, Timothy was to bring Mark when he came.

3. *Tychicus have I sent to Ephesus.* This may be rendered, "I am sending Tychicus to Ephesus." Very possibly Tychicus carried this letter to Ephesus and was to relieve Timothy in order for him to visit Paul.

The apostle also refers to personal property: his cloak, scrolls, and parchments. Timothy is to bring these with him. The *cloak* was a large mantle or long shawl. It would help Paul cope with the cold damp atmosphere of his prison cell. The *scrolls* were of papyrus, whereas the *parchments* were made from animal skins (vellum). The latter may have been leather scrolls of Old Testament Books, although this is only speculation. The parchments were much more expensive than papyrus scrolls or codices (books). Some suggest the parchments were Paul's official papers such as his certificate of Roman citizenship, etc. He had left them with Carpus in Troas which may mean Paul had been arrested suddenly and hadn't had opportunity to return for them.

## An Obstinate Opponent

"Alexander the coppersmith did me much evil:... for he hath greatly withstood our words" (vv. 14, 15). Very little is known about this Alexander. The name is used in two other references (Acts 19:33 and 1 Timothy 1:20). It is uncertain if these two Alexanders can be linked with the one mentioned here. It is not stated what Alexander did to Paul. The only clue is in the words *did me much evil* and *greatly withstood our words*. This might mean Alexander had argued with Paul when he sought to teach other Christians. Or it may mean Alexander had testified against Paul at his trial. At any rate, Paul has two other words to say about Alexander.

First, "The Lord will repay him for what he has done" (v. 14, *New International Version*). This is a prediction of punishment. Paul is willing to leave Alexander's punishment with the Lord. Here is a lesson for us: if someone has done evil against us, let us leave it with the Lord to "repay" that evil. God is the Judge; He will do all things with justice.

Second, Timothy is to be on his guard against this enemy of the gospel. The literal meaning of *be thou ware* is "be on guard" and "keep yourself away." Avoidance isn't always a sign of cowardice; often it is the better part of wisdom.

## "The Lord Stood With Me"

"At my first answer" (v. 16) probably refers to Paul's preliminary hearing before the formal trial. That "no man stood with" him could be explained by the fact that Roman Christians were not acquainted with Paul's missionary ministry, hence they could not appear as witnesses for the defense. But Paul also writes, "All men forsook me." He didn't hold it against those who deserted him, but forgave them with the words, "I pray God that it may not be laid to their charge."

But Paul did not lack support. "The Lord stood with me, and strengthened me [infused me with strength, empowered me]." Though no one else stood with Paul, the Lord did. And that's all he needed!

Paul was looking to the future when he said, "And the Lord shall deliver me from every evil work, and will preserve me unto his heavenly kingdom." Paul's thought of physical deliverance (v. 17) prompted his hope for spiritual deliverance (v. 18). So taken up with this truth of spiritual deliverance and preservation was Paul, that he burst forth in praise to God: "To whom be glory for ever and ever. Amen." What a focus the apostle Paul maintained! No matter what his circumstances, he kept his eyes on the Lord. He took courage from God's presence and placed hope in His promises.

## Final Greetings

The last verses of this letter to Timothy include the names of nine co-workers, some in Ephesus with Timothy, some in Rome, and two elsewhere. Salutations are extended to:

1. *Priscilla and Aquila.* This couple had assisted Paul in Corinth and accompanied him to Ephesus (Acts 18: 2, 3, 18, 19). They had instructed Apollos, increasing his effectiveness in the gospel (Acts 18:26). Later, they had held "church" in their own home. (See 1 Corinthians 16:19.) In Paul's letter to the Romans he tells of the time Priscilla and Aquila risked their lives for him (Romans 16:3, 4). Evidently they were now residing in Ephesus and Paul sends them greetings.

2. *Onesiphorus.* This is the second reference to the house or household of this man. Paul had commended Onesiphorus with extremely kind words in chapter 1, verses 16 and 17. Now Paul asks Timothy to "salute" Onesiphorus and his household.

Next Paul gives information about two colaborers:

3. *Erastus.* There is an Erastus mentioned in Romans 16:23 who was city treasurer or director of public works. Another Erastus was Paul's helper in Ephesus (Acts 19:22). Although we cannot be certain of the identity of the man named here, Timothy knew him and would be interested in his whereabouts.

4. *Trophimus.* This colaborer was left sick in Miletus. He is mentioned in Acts 20:4 as one among the group with Paul that collected offerings from the gentile churches to provide help for the poor saints in the Jerusalem church.

Four unknown disciples in the church at Rome are mentioned: Eubulus, Pudens, Linus, and Claudia. Then Paul adds "and all the brethren." None of these is mentioned elsewhere in Scripture. We know from Irenaeus, an Early Church father, that Linus was the first bishop of Rome.

The benediction of verse 22 is in two parts. "The Lord

Jesus Christ be with thy spirit" is directed personally to Timothy. The word *thy* is singular. But the second part, "Grace be with you," is for all Christians. The word *you* is plural. As Paul began this letter (and all his letters) with the salutation of grace (see 1:2), so he ends this final letter with a message for all. The last recorded words from one of God's greatest servants are: "Grace be with you [all]. Amen."